JELL-O®
BRAND

Tips & Techniques

All of the recipes appearing in this publication have been developed and tested by the food professionals in the JELL-O Test Kitchens. We also share our JELL-O secrets with you. These foolproof tips, many with step-by-step photos, help you get perfect results every time.

GELATIN

Making JELL-O Brand Gelatin Dessert is easy. Just follow the package directions and the results will be a success. The basic directions as written below are also on the package:

- Stir 1 cup boiling water into 1 package (4-serving size) gelatin at least 2 minutes until completely dissolved. Stir in 1 cup cold water. Refrigerate 4 hours or until firm. (For an 8-serving size package, use 2 cups boiling water and 2 cups cold water.)

- JELL-O Brand Sugar Free Low Calorie Gelatin Dessert is prepared in the same way. It can be used in many recipes that call for JELL-O Brand Gelatin Dessert.

Some tips for success

- To make a mixture that is clear and uniformly set, be sure the gelatin is completely dissolved in boiling water or other boiling liquid before adding the cold water.

- To double a recipe, just double the amounts of gelatin, liquid and other ingredients used, except salt, vinegar and lemon juice. For each of these, use 1½ times the amount given in the recipe.

- To store prepared gelatin overnight or longer, cover it before refrigerating, to prevent drying. Always store gelatin desserts and molds in the refrigerator.

- Generally, gelatin molds are best served right from the refrigerator. A gelatin mold containing fruit or vegetables can remain at room temperature up to 2 hours. Always keep a gelatin mold containing meat, mayonnaise, ice cream or other dairy products refrigerated until ready to serve. Also, do not let it sit at room temperature longer than 30 minutes. Store any leftover gelatin mold in the refrigerator.

COLLECTION

BARNES & NOBLE BOOKS

NEW YORK

This edition published by Barnes & Noble, Inc., by arrangement with Publications International, Ltd.

2005 Barnes & Noble Books

M 10 9 8 7 6 5 4 3 2 1

ISBN: 0-7607-7132-4

ANGEL FLAKE, BAKER'S, BREAKSTONE'S, COOL WHIP, COOL WHIP FREE, COOL WHIP LITE, COUNTRY TIME, GENERAL FOODS INTERNATIONAL COFFEES, HONEY MAID, JELL-O, JET-PUFFED, LORNA DOONE, MAXWELL HOUSE, MIRACLE WHIP, NABISCO, NILLA, NUTTER BUTTER, OREO, PHILADELPHIA, PLANTERS COCKTAIL and RITZ are registered trademarks of Kraft Foods Holdings.

BISQUICK is a registered trademark of General Mills, Inc.

BREYERS® is a registered trademark owned and licensed by Unilever, N.V.

DOLE® is a registered trademark of Dole Food Company, Inc.

Library of Congress Control Number: 2005920764

Microwave Cooking: Microwave ovens vary in wattage. Use the cooking times as guidelines and check for doneness before adding more time.

Preparation/Cooking Times: Preparation times are based on the approximate amount of time required to assemble the recipe before cooking, baking, chilling or serving. These times include preparation steps such as measuring, chopping and mixing. The fact that some preparations and cooking can be done simultaneously is taken into account. Preparation of optional ingredients and serving suggestions is not included.

Pictured on the front cover *(clockwise from top left):* Creamy Vanilla Sauce *(page 42),* Crown Jewel Dessert *(page 62),* Pudding Poke Cake *(page 40)* and Quick and Easy Holiday Trifle *(page 188).*

Pictured on the back cover: Peach Melba Dessert *(page 46).*

Manufactured in China.

Gelatin Consistencies

Gelatin should be consistency of thick syrup.

Set but not firm gelatin should stick to finger when touched and should mound or move to the side when bowl or mold is tilted.

Slightly thickened gelatin should be consistency of unbeaten egg whites.

Firm gelatin should not stick to finger when touched and should not move when mold is tilted.

Thickened gelatin should be thick enough for a spoon drawn through it to leave a definite impression.

Tips & Techniques

How to Speed Up Refrigerating Time

- Choose the right container. Use a metal bowl or mold rather than glass, plastic or china. Metal chills more quickly, and the gelatin will be firm in less time than in glass or plastic bowls.

- Use the speed set (ice cube) method. (Do not use this method if you are going to mold gelatin.) For a 4-serving size package, stir ¾ cup boiling water into gelatin in medium bowl at least 2 minutes until completely dissolved. Mix ½ cup cold water and ice cubes to make 1¼ cups. Add to gelatin, stirring until slightly thickened. Remove any remaining ice. Refrigerate 30 minutes for a soft set or 1 to 1½ hours until firm. (For an 8-serving size package, use 1½ cups boiling water. Mix 1 cup cold water and ice cubes to make 2½ cups.)

- Use the ice bath method. (This method will speed up the preparation of layered gelatin molds.) Prepare gelatin as directed on package. Place the bowl of gelatin in a larger bowl of ice and water. Stir occasionally as mixture chills, to ensure even thickening.

- Use the blender method. (This method can be used to make quick and easy layered gelatin desserts.) Place 1 package (4-serving size) gelatin and ¾ cup boiling liquid in blender container; cover. Blend on low speed 30 seconds. Mix ½ cup cold water and ice cubes to make 1¼ cups. Add to gelatin, stirring until partially melted; cover. Blend on low speed 30 seconds. Pour into dessert dishes. Refrigerate at least 30 minutes or until set. The mixture sets with a frothy layer on top and a clear layer on bottom. (Use this method for a 4-serving size package only. The volume of liquid required for an 8-serving size package is too large for most blenders.)

The Secret to Molding Gelatin

The Mold
- Use metal molds, plastic molds, or traditional decorative molds and other metal forms. You can use square or round cake pans, fluted or plain tube pans, loaf pans, or metal mixing bowls (the nested sets give you a variety of sizes). You can also use metal fruit or juice cans. (To unmold, dip can in warm water, then puncture bottom of can and unmold.)

- To determine the volume of the mold, measure first with water. Most recipes give an indication of the size of the mold needed. For clear gelatin, you need a 2-cup mold for a 4-serving size package and a 4-cup mold for an 8-serving size package.

- If the mold holds less than the size called for, pour the extra gelatin into a separate dish. Refrigerate and serve it at another time. Do not use a mold that is too large, since it would be difficult to unmold. Either increase the recipe or use a smaller mold.

- For easier unmolding, spray the mold with no stick cooking spray before filling it.

Gelatin Refrigerating Time Chart

In all recipes, for best results, the gelatin needs to be refrigerated to the proper consistency. Use this chart as a guideline to determine the desired consistency and the approximate refrigerating time.

When a recipe says:	It means gelatin should:	Refrigerating Time:		Gelatin Uses:
		Regular set	Speed set*	
"Refrigerate until syrupy"	Be consistency of thick syrup	1 hour	3 minutes	Glaze for pies, fruit
"Refrigerate until slightly thickened"	Be consistency of unbeaten egg whites	1¼ hours	5 to 6 minutes	Adding creamy ingredients or when mixture will be beaten
"Refrigerate until thickened"	Be thick enough so that a spoon drawn through leaves a definite impression	1½ hours	7 to 8 minutes	Adding solid ingredients such as fruits or vegetables
"Refrigerate until set but not firm"	Stick to finger when touched and should mound or move to the side when bowl or mold is tilted	2 hours	30 minutes	Layering gelatin mixtures
"Refrigerate until firm"	Not stick to finger when touched and not mound or move when mold is tilted	Individual molds: at least 3 hours / 2- to 6-cup mold: at least 4 hours / 8- to 12-cup mold: at least 5 hours or overnight		Unmolding and serving

*Speed set (ice cube) method is not recommended for molding.

The Preparation

- To prepare gelatin for molding, use less water than the amount called for on the package. For a 4-serving size package, decrease cold water to ¾ cup. For an 8-serving size package, decrease to 1½ cups. (This adjustment has already been made in the recipes.) The firmer consistency will result in a less fragile mold and will make unmolding much simpler.

- To arrange fruits or vegetables in the mold, refrigerate gelatin until thickened. (If gelatin is not thick enough, fruits or vegetables may sink or float.) Pour gelatin into mold to about ¼-inch depth. Reserve remaining gelatin at room temperature. Arrange fruits or vegetables in decorative pattern on gelatin. Refrigerate until gelatin is set but not firm. Spoon reserved gelatin over pattern in mold. Refrigerate until firm, then unmold.

The Unmolding

- First, allow gelatin to set until firm by refrigerating several hours or overnight. Chill serving plate in refrigerator, as well.

- Make certain gelatin is completely firm. It should not feel sticky on top and should not mound or move to the side if mold is tilted.

- Moisten tips of fingers and gently pull gelatin from around edge of mold.

Tips & Techniques

- Or, use a small metal spatula or pointed knife dipped in warm water to loosen top edge.

- Dip mold in warm, not hot, water just to rim for about 15 seconds. Lift from water, hold upright and shake to loosen gelatin. Or, gently pull gelatin from edge of mold.

- Moisten chilled serving plate with water. (This allows gelatin to be moved after unmolding.) Place moistened serving plate on top of mold. Invert mold and plate; holding mold and plate together, shake slightly to loosen. Gently remove mold. If gelatin does not release easily, dip mold in warm water again for a few seconds. Center gelatin on serving plate.

Unmolding

1. Before unmolding, gently pull gelatin from around edge of mold with moistened fingertips.

4. Place moistened serving plate on top of mold.

2. Dip mold in warm water, just to the rim, for about 15 seconds.

5. Invert mold and plate; shake to loosen gelatin.

3. Lift mold from water; hold upright. Shake to loosen gelatin.

6. Remove mold and center gelatin on plate.

PUDDING

The recipes use both JELL-O Cook & Serve Pudding & Pie Filling (requires cooking) and JELL-O Instant Pudding & Pie Filling (not cooked.) These products are not interchangeable. Be sure to use the product called for in the recipe. JELL-O Instant Pudding & Pie Filling is also available Fat Free. Both the Instant and the Cook & Serve Pudding & Pie Fillings are also available as Fat Free Sugar Free.

See individual packages for basic directions for preparing the products as either a pudding or a pie filling.

Some Tips for Success

For JELL-O Instant Pudding & Pie Filling
- Always use cold milk. Beat pudding mix slowly, not vigorously.

- For best results, use 2% lowfat milk or whole milk. Skim, 1% lowfat, reconstituted nonfat dry milk or lactose-reduced milk can also be used. For Fat Free or Fat Free Sugar Free Pudding & Pie Filling, use cold skim milk.

- Always store prepared pudding desserts, pies and snacks in the refrigerator.

For JELL-O Cook & Serve Pudding & Pie Filling
- It's best to cook the pudding in a heavy saucepan to ensure even heating. Stir pudding mixture constantly as it cooks. Make sure it comes to full boil. The mixture will be thin, but will thicken as it cools.

- For a creamier pudding, place a piece of plastic wrap on the surface of pudding while cooling. Stir before serving.

- To cool pudding quickly, place saucepan of hot pudding in larger pan of ice water; stir frequently until mixture is cooled. Do not use this method for pie filling.

NO BAKE CHEESECAKES and DESSERTS

Some Tips for Success
- The cheesecake can be prepared in an 8- or 9-inch square pan or 12 foil- or paper-lined muffin cups.

- Two packages of the cheesecake can be prepared in a 13×9-inch pan or a 9×3-inch springform pan.

- To serve, dip the pan to the rim in hot water for 30 seconds before cutting.

- To freeze, cover the cheesecake. Freeze up to 2 weeks. Thaw in refrigerator 3 hours before serving.

- For easy cleanup, line the 8- or 9-inch square pan with foil before preparing the No Bake Dessert.

- The No Bake Desserts can also be served frozen. Freeze 4 hours or until firm. Remove from freezer and serve immediately.

JELL-O®

BRAND

Shimmering Shapes

Rainbow Ribbon Mold

Prep Time: 1 hour   **Refrigerating Time:** 4½ hours

6¼ cups boiling water
5 packages (4-serving size) JELL-O® Brand Gelatin Dessert, any 5 different flavors
1 cup (½ pint) BREAKSTONE'S® Sour Cream or BREYERS® Vanilla Lowfat Yogurt

STIR 1¼ cups boiling water into 1 flavor of gelatin in small bowl at least 2 minutes until completely dissolved. Pour ¾ cup of the dissolved gelatin into 6-cup ring mold. Refrigerate about 15 minutes until set but not firm (gelatin should stick to finger when touched and should mound). Refrigerate remaining gelatin in bowl about 5 minutes until slightly thickened (consistency of unbeaten egg whites). Gradually stir in 3 tablespoons of the sour cream. Spoon over gelatin in pan. Refrigerate about 15 minutes or until set but not firm (gelatin should stick to finger when touched and should mound).

MEANWHILE, repeat process with each remaining gelatin flavor. (Be sure to cool dissolved gelatin to room temperature before pouring into mold.) Refrigerate gelatin as directed to create a total of 10 alternating clear and creamy gelatin layers.

REFRIGERATE 2 hours or until firm. Unmold. Garnish as desired.

Makes 12 servings

11

Shimmering Shapes

Sparkling Berry Salad

Prep Time: 15 minutes   **Refrigerating Time:** 5½ hours

> **2 cups** boiling diet cranberry juice cocktail
> **1 package** (8-serving size) or **2 packages** (4-serving size each)
>   JELL-O® Brand Sugar Free Low Calorie Gelatin Dessert
>   or JELL-O® Brand Gelatin Dessert, any red flavor
> **1½ cups** cold seltzer or club soda
> **¼ cup** creme de cassis liqueur (optional)
> **1 teaspoon** lemon juice
> **3 cups** assorted berries (blueberries, raspberries and sliced
>   strawberries), divided

STIR boiling cranberry juice into gelatin in large bowl at least 2 minutes until completely dissolved. Stir in cold seltzer, liqueur and lemon juice. Refrigerate about 1½ hours or until slightly thickened (consistency of unbeaten egg whites).

STIR in 2 cups of the berries. Spoon into 5-cup mold.

REFRIGERATE 4 hours or until firm. Unmold. Top with remaining 1 cup berries.   **Makes 8 servings**

Tip

Fruit should be added to gelatin that has been chilled until it thickens, but is not yet set. This way the fruit will remain suspended in the gelatin.

Shimmering Shapes

Orange Mousse with Strawberry Sauce

Prep Time: 15 minutes plus refrigerating

> 1½ cups boiling water
> 1 package (8-serving size) or 2 packages (4-serving size each) JELL-O® Brand Orange Flavor Gelatin
> 2 teaspoons grated orange peel (optional)
> 1 cup cold water
> ¾ cup cold orange juice
> 1 tub (8 ounces) COOL WHIP® Whipped Topping, thawed
> 1 package (10 ounces) frozen strawberries or raspberries in syrup, thawed, puréed in blender

STIR boiling water into gelatin and orange peel in large bowl at least 2 minutes until gelatin is completely dissolved. Stir in cold water and orange juice. Refrigerate about 1¼ hours or until slightly thickened (consistency of unbeaten egg whites).

STIR in whipped topping with wire whisk until smooth. Pour into 6-cup mold which has been sprayed with no stick cooking spray.

REFRIGERATE 3 hours or until firm. Unmold. Serve with puréed strawberries.   **Makes 12 servings**

For individual servings: Pour mousse mixture into 12 (6-ounce) custard cups, filling each about ¾ full.

Lemon Mousse: Substitute JELL-O® Brand Lemon Flavor Gelatin and lemon peel for the Orange Flavor Gelatin and orange peel.

Shimmering Shapes

Juice 'n Fruit Salad

Prep Time: 20 minutes   **Refrigerating Time:** 6 hours

2 cups boiling water, divided
**1 package (4-serving size) JELL-O® Brand Gelatin, any red
flavor**
1 cup cold orange juice, divided
1 can (8 ounces) sliced peaches, drained, chopped
**1 package (4-serving size) JELL-O® Brand Orange Flavor
Gelatin**
1 can (8 ounces) crushed pineapple, drained

STIR 1 cup of the boiling water into red gelatin in medium bowl at least
2 minutes until completely dissolved. Stir in ½ cup of the cold juice.
Refrigerate about 45 minutes or until slightly thickened (consistency of
unbeaten egg whites). Stir in peaches. Spoon into 5-cup mold which has
been sprayed with no stick cooking spray. Refrigerate about 20 minutes or
until set but not firm (should stick to finger when touched and should
mound).

MEANWHILE, stir remaining 1 cup boiling water into orange gelatin in
medium bowl at least 2 minutes until completely dissolved. Stir in remaining
½ cup cold juice. Refrigerate about 45 minutes or until slightly thickened.
Stir in pineapple. Spoon over red gelatin in mold.

REFRIGERATE 4 hours or until firm. Unmold. Garnish as desired.

Makes 10 servings

Spiced Cranberry Orange Mold

Prep Time: 20 minutes   **Refrigerating Time:** 5½ hours

  1½ **cups boiling water**
   1 **package (8-serving size) or 2 packages (4-serving size each)**
       JELL-O® Brand Cranberry Flavor Gelatin, or any red flavor
   1 **can (16 ounces) whole berry cranberry sauce**
   1 **cup cold water**
   1 **tablespoon lemon juice**
  ¼ **teaspoon ground cinnamon**
  ⅛ **teaspoon ground cloves**
   1 **orange, sectioned, diced**
  ½ **cup chopped walnuts**

STIR boiling water into gelatin in large bowl at least 2 minutes until completely dissolved. Stir in cranberry sauce, cold water, lemon juice, cinnamon and cloves. Refrigerate about 1½ hours or until thickened (spoon drawn through leaves definite impression).

STIR in orange and walnuts. Spoon into 5-cup mold.

REFRIGERATE 4 hours or until firm. Unmold. Garnish as desired.

Makes 10 servings

Apple Blossom Mold

Prep Time: 15 minutes   **Refrigerating Time:** 5½ hours

 1½ **cups boiling water**
   1 **package (8-serving size) or 2 packages (4-serving size each)**
      JELL-O® Brand Lemon Flavor Gelatin
   2 **cups cold apple juice**
   1 **cup diced red and green apples**

STIR boiling water into gelatin in large bowl at least 2 minutes until completely dissolved. Stir in cold juice. Refrigerate about 1½ hours or until thickened (spoon drawn through leaves definite impression). Stir in apples. Pour into 6-cup mold which has been sprayed with no stick cooking spray.

REFRIGERATE 4 hours or until firm. Unmold. Garnish as desired.

Makes 10 servings

Tip

Sugar Free Low Calorie Gelatin may be substituted.

Shimmering Shapes

Melon Salad

Prep Time: 15 minutes   **Refrigerating Time:** 5½ hours

  2½ **cups boiling apple juice**
    1 **package (8-serving size) or 2 packages (4-serving size each)**
        JELL-O® Brand Watermelon Flavor Sugar Free Low Calorie
        Gelatin Dessert or JELL-O® Brand Watermelon Flavor
        Gelatin Dessert
  1½ **cups cold seltzer or club soda**
    1 **teaspoon lemon juice**
    2 **cups cantaloupe and honeydew melon cubes**

STIR boiling juice into gelatin in large bowl at least 2 minutes until completely dissolved. Stir in cold seltzer and lemon juice. Refrigerate about 1½ hours or until thickened (spoon drawn through leaves definite impression). Stir in melon cubes. Spoon into 6-cup mold.

REFRIGERATE 4 hours or until firm. Unmold. Garnish as desired.

Makes 10 servings

Strawberry Banana Salad

Prep Time: 15 minutes   **Refrigerating Time:** 5½ hours

  1½ **cups boiling water**
    1 **package (8-serving size) or 2 packages (4-serving size each)**
        JELL-O® Brand Strawberry or Strawberry Banana Flavor
        Sugar Free Low Calorie Gelatin
    2 **cups cold water**
    1 **cup chopped strawberries**
    1 **banana, sliced**

STIR boiling water into gelatin in large bowl at least 2 minutes until completely dissolved. Stir in cold water. Refrigerate about 1½ hours or until thickened (spoon drawn through leaves definite impression).

STIR in strawberries and banana. Pour into 5-cup mold that has been sprayed with no stick cooking spray.

REFRIGERATE 4 hours or until firm. Unmold. Store leftover gelatin mold in refrigerator.

Makes 10 (½-cup) servings

Shimmering Shapes

Peaches and Cream Mold

Prep Time: 15 minutes   **Refrigerating Time:** 5½ hours

   1½ cups boiling water
   **1 package (8-serving size) or 2 packages (4-serving size each)
     JELL-O® Brand Peach or Orange Flavor Gelatin**
   1½ cups cold water
   **1 tub (8 ounces) COOL WHIP® Whipped Topping, thawed,
     divided**
   1 can (16 ounces) peach slices in syrup, drained, diced

STIR boiling water into gelatin in large bowl at least 2 minutes until completely dissolved. Stir in cold water. Refrigerate about 1¼ hours or until slightly thickened (consistency of unbeaten egg whites).

STIR in 2 cups whipped topping with wire whisk until smooth. Refrigerate about 15 minutes or until thickened (spoon drawn through leaves definite impression). Stir in peaches. Pour into 5-cup mold which has been sprayed with no stick cooking spray.

REFRIGERATE 4 hours or until firm. Unmold. Garnish as desired. Serve with remaining whipped topping.   **Makes 10 servings**

Sparkling Tropical Fruit Mold

Prep Time: 15 minutes   **Refrigerating Time:** 4¾ hours

   1½ cups boiling white grape juice
   **1 package (6 ounces) or 2 packages (3 ounces each) JELL-O®
     Brand Sparkling White Grape Flavor Gelatin**
   2 cups cold club soda or seltzer
   1 can (15.25 ounces) tropical fruit salad, drained, chopped
   ½ cup dried cranberries

STIR boiling juice into gelatin in large bowl at least 2 minutes until completely dissolved. Refrigerate 15 minutes. Gently stir in cold club soda. Refrigerate 30 minutes or until slightly thickened (consistency of unbeaten egg whites). Gently stir tropical fruit salad and cranberries into gelatin. Spoon into 6-cup mold which has been sprayed with no stick cooking spray; cover.

REFRIGERATE 4 hours or until firm. Unmold. Garnish as desired.

                                        Makes 12 servings

Lemon Mousse with Raspberry Sauce

Prep Time: 15 minutes   **Refrigerating Time:** 4¼ hours

> 1½ **cups boiling water**
> 1 **package (8-serving size) or 2 packages (4-serving size each)**
> **JELL-O® Brand Lemon Flavor Gelatin Dessert**
> 2 **teaspoons grated lemon peel**
> 1 **cup cold water**
> ¾ **cup cold orange juice**
> 1 **tub (8 ounces) COOL WHIP® Whipped Topping, thawed**
> 1 **package (10 ounces) frozen raspberries or strawberries in**
> **syrup, thawed, puréed in blender**

STIR boiling water into gelatin and lemon peel in large bowl at least 2 minutes until gelatin is completely dissolved. Stir in cold water and orange juice. Refrigerate about 1¼ hours or until slightly thickened (consistency of unbeaten egg whites).

STIR in whipped topping with wire whisk until smooth. Pour into 12 (6-ounce) custard cups, filling each about ¾ full. (Or, pour into 6-cup mold.)

REFRIGERATE 3 hours or until firm. Unmold. Serve with raspberry sauce.

Makes 12 servings

Variation: Apple juice may be substituted for the orange juice.

Mimosa Mold

Prep Time: 15 minutes   **Refrigerating Time:** 4¾ hours

  1½ cups boiling water
    1 package (8-serving size) or 2 packages (4-serving size each)
      JELL-O® Brand Sparkling White Grape or Lemon Flavor
      Gelatin Dessert
    2 cups cold seltzer or club soda
    1 can (11 ounces) mandarin orange segments, drained
    1 cup sliced strawberries

STIR boiling water into gelatin in large bowl at least 2 minutes or until completely dissolved. Refrigerate 15 minutes. Gently stir in seltzer. Refrigerate about 30 minutes or until slightly thickened (consistency of unbeaten egg whites). Gently stir about 15 seconds. Stir in oranges and strawberries. Pour into 6-cup mold.

REFRIGERATE 4 hours or until firm. Unmold. Garnish as desired. Store leftover gelatin mold in refrigerator.   **Makes 12 servings**

Layered Pear Cream Cheese Mold

Prep Time: 30 minutes   **Refrigerating Time:** 5 hours

1 can (16 ounces) pear halves, undrained
1 package (8-serving size) or 2 packages (4-serving size each)
    JELL-O® Brand Lime Flavor Gelatin Dessert
1 ½ cups cold ginger ale or water
2 tablespoons lemon juice
1 package (8 ounces) PHILADELPHIA® Cream Cheese, softened
¼ cup chopped pecans

DRAIN pears, reserving liquid. Dice pears; set aside. Add water to liquid to make 1½ cups; bring to boil in small saucepan.

STIR boiling liquid into gelatin in large bowl at least 2 minutes until completely dissolved. Stir in cold ginger ale and lemon juice. Reserve 2½ cups gelatin at room temperature. Pour remaining gelatin into 5-cup mold. Refrigerate about 30 minutes or until thickened (spoon drawn through leaves definite impression). Arrange about ½ cup of the diced pears in thickened gelatin in mold.

STIR reserved 2½ cups gelatin gradually into cream cheese in large bowl with wire whisk until smooth. Refrigerate about 30 minutes or until slightly thickened (consistency of unbeaten egg whites). Stir in remaining diced pears and pecans. Spoon over gelatin layer in mold.

REFRIGERATE 4 hours or until firm. Unmold. Garnish as desired.

Makes 10 servings

Shimmering Shapes

Sunset Yogurt Mold

Prep Time: 20 minutes   **Refrigerating Time:** 6 hours

> **2 cups boiling water**
> **1 package (8-serving size) or 2 packages (4-serving size each) JELL-O® Brand Orange Flavor Sugar Free Low Calorie Gelatin Dessert or JELL-O® Brand Orange Flavor Gelatin Dessert**
> **¼ cup cold water**
> **1 can (8 ounces) crushed pineapple in juice, undrained**
> **1 cup grated carrots**
> **1 container (8 ounces) BREYERS® Vanilla Lowfat Yogurt**

STIR boiling water into gelatin in large bowl at least 2 minutes until completely dissolved. Reserve 1 cup gelatin at room temperature. Stir cold water, pineapple with juice and carrots into remaining gelatin. Spoon into 5-cup mold. Refrigerate about 2 hours or until set but not firm (gelatin should stick to finger when touched and should mound).

STIR yogurt into reserved 1 cup gelatin with wire whisk until smooth. Pour over gelatin layer in mold.

REFRIGERATE 4 hours or until firm. Unmold.   **Makes 10 servings**

Mandarin Orange Mold

Prep Time: 20 minutes   **Refrigerating Time:** 6 hours

> **2 cups boiling water**
> **1 package (8-serving size) or 2 packages (4-serving size each) JELL-O® Brand Orange Flavor Sugar Free Low Calorie Gelatin Dessert or JELL-O® Brand Orange Flavor Gelatin Dessert**
> **¾ cup cold water**
> **1 can (11 ounces) mandarin orange segments in juice, drained**
> **1 container (8 ounces) BREYERS® Vanilla Lowfat Yogurt**

STIR boiling water into gelatin in large bowl at least 2 minutes until completely dissolved. Reserve 1 cup gelatin at room temperature. Stir cold water and oranges into remaining gelatin. Pour into 5-cup mold. Refrigerate about 2 hours until set but not firm (gelatin should stick to finger when touched and should mound).

STIR yogurt into reserved 1 cup gelatin with wire whisk until smooth. Pour over gelatin layer in mold.

REFRIGERATE 4 hours or until firm. Unmold.   **Makes 10 servings**

Under-the-Sea Salad

Prep Time: 20 minutes   **Refrigerating Time:** 5 hours

> **1 can (16 ounces) pear halves in syrup, undrained**
> **1 cup boiling water**
> **1 package (4-serving size) JELL-O® Brand Lime Flavor Gelatin Dessert**
> **¼ teaspoon salt (optional)**
> **1 tablespoon lemon juice**
> **3 packages (3 ounces each) PHILADELPHIA® Cream Cheese, softened**
> **⅛ teaspoon ground cinnamon (optional)**

DRAIN pears, reserving ¾ cup of the syrup. Dice pears; set aside.

STIR boiling water into gelatin and salt in medium bowl at least 2 minutes until completely dissolved. Stir in reserved syrup and lemon juice. Pour 1 ¼ cups gelatin into 4-cup mold or 8×4-inch loaf pan. Refrigerate about 1 hour or until set but not firm (gelatin should stick to finger when touched and should mound).

MEANWHILE, stir remaining gelatin gradually into cream cheese in large bowl with wire whisk until smooth. Stir in pears and cinnamon. Spoon over gelatin layer in mold.

REFRIGERATE 4 hours or until firm. Unmold. Garnish as desired.

Makes 6 servings

Tip

Soften cream cheese quickly by removing it from its wrapper, placing it in a medium microwave-safe bowl, and microwaving on MEDIUM (50% power) 15 to 20 seconds or until slightly softened.

Cranberry Cream Cheese Mold

Prep Time: 20 minutes   **Refrigerating Time:** 6 hours

> 1 ½ **cups boiling water**
>   1 **package (8-serving size) or 2 packages (4-serving size each)**
>   **JELL-O® Brand Cranberry Flavor Gelatin Dessert, or any**
>   **red flavor**
> 1 ½ **cups cold water**
>   ½ **teaspoon ground cinnamon**
>   1 **medium apple, chopped**
>   1 **cup whole berry cranberry sauce**
>   1 **package (8 ounces) PHILADELPHIA® Cream Cheese, softened**

STIR boiling water into gelatin in large bowl at least 2 minutes until completely dissolved. Stir in cold water and cinnamon. Reserve 1 cup gelatin at room temperature. Refrigerate remaining gelatin about 1 ½ hours or until thickened (spoon drawn through leaves definite impression).

STIR apple and cranberry sauce into thickened gelatin. Spoon into 6-cup mold. Refrigerate about 30 minutes or until set but not firm (gelatin should stick to finger when touched and should mound).

STIR reserved 1 cup gelatin gradually into cream cheese in medium bowl with wire whisk until smooth. Pour over gelatin layer in mold.

REFRIGERATE 4 hours or until firm. Unmold. Garnish as desired.

Makes 12 servings

Note: To prepare without cream cheese layer, omit cream cheese. Refrigerate all of the gelatin about 1 ½ hours or until thickened. Stir in apple and cranberry sauce. Pour into mold. Refrigerate.

Clockwise from top: **Cranberry Cream Cheese Mold, White Sangria Splash** (page 32), **Cucumber Sour Cream Mold** (page 32) and **Sunset Fruit Salad** (page 33)

White Sangria Splash

Prep Time: 15 minutes   **Refrigerating Time:** 4 hours

- **1 cup dry white wine**
- **1 package (8-serving size) or 2 packages (4-serving size each) JELL-O® Brand Lemon Flavor Sugar Free Low Calorie Gelatin Dessert or JELL-O® Brand Lemon Flavor Gelatin Dessert**
- **3 cups cold seltzer or club soda**
- **1 tablespoon lime juice**
- **1 tablespoon orange juice or orange liqueur**
- **3 cups seedless grapes, divided**
- **1 cup sliced strawberries**
- **1 cup whole small strawberries**

BRING wine to boil in small saucepan. Stir boiling wine into gelatin in medium bowl at least 2 minutes until completely dissolved. Stir in cold seltzer and lime and orange juices. Place bowl of gelatin in larger bowl of ice and water. Let stand about 10 minutes or until thickened (spoon drawn through leaves definite impression), stirring occasionally.

STIR in 1 cup of the grapes and the sliced strawberries. Pour into 6-cup mold.

REFRIGERATE 4 hours or until firm. Unmold. Garnish with remaining grapes and whole strawberries.   **Makes 12 servings**

Cucumber Sour Cream Mold

Prep Time: 15 minutes   **Refrigerating Time:** 5½ hours

- **1½ cups boiling water**
- **1 package (8-serving size) or 2 packages (4-serving size each) JELL-O® Brand Lime Flavor Gelatin Dessert**
- **¼ teaspoon salt**
- **1½ cups cold water**
- **1 tablespoon lemon juice**
- **½ cup MIRACLE WHIP® Salad Dressing**
- **½ cup BREAKSTONE'S® Sour Cream**
- **1½ cups chopped seeded peeled cucumber**
- **2 tablespoons minced onion**
- **1 teaspoon dill weed**

STIR boiling water into gelatin and salt in large bowl at least 2 minutes until completely dissolved. Stir in cold water and lemon juice. Refrigerate about 1¼ hours or until slightly thickened (consistency of unbeaten egg whites).

MIX salad dressing and sour cream in small bowl until well blended. Stir into thickened gelatin. Refrigerate about 15 minutes or until thickened (spoon drawn through leaves definite impression). Stir in cucumber, onion and dill weed. Pour into 5-cup mold.

REFRIGERATE 4 hours or until firm. Unmold. Garnish as desired.

Makes 10 servings

Sunset Fruit Salad

Prep Time: 20 minutes   **Refrigerating Time:** 5 hours

2 cups boiling water
1 package (4-serving size) JELL-O® Brand Cranberry Flavor Sugar Free Low Calorie Gelatin Dessert or JELL-O® Brand Cranberry Flavor Gelatin Dessert, or any red flavor
½ cup cold water
1 can (8 ounces) sliced peaches in juice, drained, chopped
1 package (4-serving size) JELL-O® Brand Orange Flavor Sugar Free Low Calorie Gelatin Dessert or JELL-O® Brand Orange Flavor Gelatin Dessert
1 can (8 ounces) crushed pineapple in juice, undrained

STIR 1 cup of the boiling water into cranberry gelatin in medium bowl at least 2 minutes until completely dissolved. Stir in cold water. Refrigerate about 45 minutes or until slightly thickened (consistency of unbeaten egg whites). Stir in peaches. Spoon into 5-cup mold. Refrigerate about 15 minutes or until set but not firm (gelatin should stick to finger when touched and should mound).

MEANWHILE, stir remaining 1 cup boiling water into orange gelatin in medium bowl at least 2 minutes until completely dissolved. Stir in pineapple with juice. Pour over gelatin layer in mold.

REFRIGERATE 4 hours or until firm. Unmold. Garnish as desired.

Makes 10 servings

JELL-O®
BRAND

Best of the Best

Creamy Fruited Mold

Prep Time: 15 minutes   **Refrigerating Time:** 5½ hours

- **1 cup boiling water**
- **1 package (4-serving size) JELL-O® Brand Gelatin Dessert, any flavor**
- **1 cup cold water or apple juice**
- **1½ cups thawed COOL WHIP® Whipped Topping**
- **1 cup diced fruit**

STIR boiling water into gelatin in medium bowl at least 2 minutes until completely dissolved. Stir in cold water. Refrigerate about 1¼ hours or until slightly thickened (consistency of unbeaten egg whites). Gently stir in whipped topping. Refrigerate about 15 minutes or until thickened (spoon drawn through leaves definite impression). Stir in fruit. Pour into 5-cup mold.

REFRIGERATE 4 hours or until firm. Unmold. Garnish as desired.

Makes 8 servings

Confetti Pie

Prep Time: 15 minutes plus refrigerating

1 cup boiling water
1 package (4-serving size) JELL-O® Brand Lemon Flavor Gelatin
½ cup cold water
1 cup boiling water
1 package (4-serving size) JELL-O® Brand Orange Flavor Gelatin
½ cup cold orange juice
2 cups thawed COOL WHIP® Whipped Topping
⅓ cup multi-colored sprinkles
1 HONEY MAID® Honey Graham Pie Crust (9 inch)

STIR 1 cup boiling water into lemon gelatin in medium bowl at least 2 minutes until completely dissolved. Stir in cold water. Pour into 8-inch square pan. Refrigerate 4 hours or until firm. Cut into ½-inch cubes.

STIR 1 cup boiling water into orange gelatin in large bowl at least 2 minutes until completely dissolved. Stir in orange juice. Refrigerate about 20 minutes or until slightly thickened (consistency of unbeaten egg whites). Gently stir in whipped topping. Gently stir in gelatin cubes and sprinkles. Refrigerate until mixture will mound. Pour into crust.

REFRIGERATE at least 4 hours or until firm. Garnish with additional whipped topping and sprinkles, if desired.   **Makes 8 servings**

Great Substitutes: Try Berry Blue or Lime Flavor Gelatin instead of Lemon Flavor when making the gelatin cubes.

Fruit 'n Juice Squares

Prep Time: 15 minutes   **Refrigerating Time:** 3¾ hours

1½ cups boiling water
1 package (8-serving size) or 2 packages (4-serving size each)
   JELL-O® Brand Strawberry or Cranberry Flavor Gelatin
1 cup cold orange juice
   Ice cubes
1 tub (8 ounces) COOL WHIP® Whipped Topping, thawed,
   divided
1 can (8¾ ounces) fruit cocktail, drained

STIR boiling water into gelatin in large bowl at least 2 minutes until completely dissolved. Mix cold juice and ice cubes to make 1¼ cups. Add to gelatin, stirring until slightly thickened (consistency of unbeaten egg whites). Remove any remaining ice. Refrigerate 45 minutes.

RESERVE 1 cup gelatin; set aside. Stir ½ of the whipped topping into remaining gelatin until smooth. Pour mixture into 8-inch square pan. Refrigerate about 5 minutes until set but not firm (should stick to finger when touched and should mound). Stir fruit into reserved gelatin and carefully spoon over creamy layer in pan.

REFRIGERATE 3 hours or until firm. Cut into squares and garnish with remaining whipped topping.   **Makes 9 servings**

Substitution: 1 cup seasonal fresh berries may be substituted for canned fruit.

Key Lime Pie

Prep Time: 15 minutes   **Refrigerating Time:** 2½ hours

> 1¾ **cups boiling water**
> 1 **package (8-serving size) or 2 packages (4-serving size each)**
>   **JELL-O® Brand Lime Flavor Gelatin Dessert**
> 2 **teaspoons grated lime peel**
> ¼ **cup lime juice**
> 1 **pint (2 cups) vanilla ice cream, softened**
> 1 **prepared graham cracker crumb crust (6 ounces)**

STIR boiling water into gelatin in large bowl at least 2 minutes until completely dissolved. Stir in lime peel and juice.

STIR in ice cream until melted and smooth. Refrigerate 15 to 20 minutes or until mixture is very thick and will mound. Spoon into crust.

REFRIGERATE 2 hours or until firm. Garnish as desired.

Makes 8 servings

Pudding Poke Cake

Prep Time: 30 minutes   **Bake Time:** 40 minutes
Refrigerating Time: 1 hour

> 1 **package (2-layer size) chocolate cake mix or cake mix with**
>   **pudding in the mix**
> 4 **cups cold milk**
> 2 **packages (4-serving size each) JELL-O® Vanilla Flavor Instant**
>   **Pudding & Pie Filling**

PREPARE and bake cake mix as directed on package for 13×9-inch baking pan. Remove from oven. Immediately poke holes at 1-inch intervals down through cake to pan with round handle of a wooden spoon. (Or poke holes with a plastic drinking straw, using turning motion to make large holes.)

POUR milk into large bowl. Add pudding mixes. Beat with wire whisk 2 minutes. Quickly pour about ½ of the thin pudding mixture evenly over warm cake and into holes. Let remaining pudding mixture stand to thicken slightly. Spoon over top of cake, swirling to frost cake.

REFRIGERATE at least 1 hour or until ready to serve.

Makes 15 servings

Dulce de Leche Frozen Dessert

Prep Time: 20 minutes   **Freeze Time:** 6 hours

3 cups half-and-half or milk
6 tablespoons KRAFT® Caramel Topping, divided
1 package (4-serving size) JELL-O® Butterscotch Flavor Instant Pudding & Pie Filling
1 package (4-serving size) JELL-O® Vanilla Flavor Instant Pudding & Pie Filling
1 tub (8 ounces) COOL WHIP® Whipped Topping, thawed

POUR half-and-half into large bowl. Stir in 2 tablespoons caramel topping until dissolved. Add pudding mixes. Beat with wire whisk 1 minute or until well blended. Gently stir in whipped topping until well mixed.

SPOON ½ of the pudding mixture into 8×4-inch loaf pan which has been lined with plastic wrap. Drizzle remaining caramel topping over mixture. Carefully spoon remaining pudding mixture over caramel and smooth with spatula.

FREEZE about 6 hours or overnight or until firm. Carefully invert pan onto serving platter and remove plastic wrap. Let stand at room temperature about 15 minutes before slicing.   **Makes 8 servings**

Variation: To prepare individual Dulce de Leche frozen pops or cups, spoon ½ of the pudding mixture into 10 to 12 paper-lined muffin cups. Place teaspoonful of caramel topping in center of each cup and cover with remaining pudding mixture. For pops, stick wooden popsicle sticks into each cup and freeze.

Creamy Vanilla Sauce

Prep Time: 5 minutes

3½ cups cold milk, light cream or half-and-half
1 package (4-serving size) JELL-O® Vanilla or French Vanilla Flavor Instant Pudding & Pie Filling

POUR milk into bowl. Add pudding mix. Beat with wire whisk 2 minutes. Cover.

REFRIGERATE until ready to serve. Serve over your favorite fruits or cake. Garnish as desired.   **Makes 8 servings**

Creamy Citrus Sauce: Add 2 teaspoons grated orange peel along with pudding mix.

Decadent Chocolate Cream Pie

Prep Time: 10 minutes plus refrigerating

**2 packages (4-serving size each) JELL-O® Chocolate Flavor
  Cook & Serve Pudding & Pie Filling (not Instant)**
3½ cups half-and-half
1 baked pastry shell (9 inch), cooled
1 tub (8 ounces) COOL WHIP® Whipped Topping, thawed

STIR pudding mixes and half-and-half in medium saucepan with wire whisk until blended. Stirring constantly, cook over medium heat until mixture comes to full boil. Pour into pastry shell.

REFRIGERATE 3 hours or until set. Garnish pie with whipped topping.

Makes 8 servings

Great Substitute: Use an OREO Pie Crust (9 inch) instead of a pastry shell. Garnish pie with chocolate shavings or chocolate sprinkles.

Baked Custard Fruit Tart

Prep Time: 10 minutes   **Bake Time:** 45 minutes

2 teaspoons sugar
1½ cups milk
2 eggs
2 tablespoons flour
**1 package (4-serving size) JELL-O® Vanilla Flavor Cook
  & Serve Pudding & Pie Filling (not instant)**
1 can (15 ounces) sliced peaches, drained

HEAT oven to 350°F. Grease 9-inch pie plate; sprinkle with sugar.

BEAT milk, eggs, flour and pudding mix until well mixed. Pour into prepared pie plate. Arrange peaches in pudding mixture.

BAKE 40 to 45 minutes or until filling is set and surface is golden brown. Cool on wire rack. Serve warm or cold, with whipped topping, if desired.

Makes 8 servings

Lemon Chiffon Pie

Prep Time: 20 minutes   **Refrigerating Time:** 6½ hours

- **⅔ cup boiling water**
- **1 package (4-serving size) JELL-O® Brand Lemon Flavor Gelatin Dessert**
- **2 teaspoons grated lemon peel**
- **2 tablespoons lemon juice**
- **½ cup cold water**
- **Ice cubes**
- **1 tub (8 ounces) COOL WHIP® Whipped Topping, thawed**
- **1 prepared graham cracker crumb crust (6 ounces)**

STIR boiling water into gelatin in large bowl at least 2 minutes or until completely dissolved. Stir in lemon peel and juice. Mix cold water and ice to make 1¼ cups. Add to gelatin, stirring until slightly thickened. Remove any remaining ice.

STIR in whipped topping with wire whisk until smooth. Refrigerate 20 to 30 minutes or until mixture is very thick and will mound. Spoon into crust.

REFRIGERATE 6 hours or overnight until firm. Garnish as desired.

Makes 8 servings

Watergate Salad (Pistachio Pineapple Delight)

Prep Time: 10 minutes   **Refrigerating Time:** 1 hour

- **1 package (4-serving size) JELL-O® Pistachio Flavor Instant Pudding & Pie Filling**
- **1 can (20 ounces) crushed pineapple in juice, undrained**
- **1 cup miniature marshmallows**
- **½ cup chopped nuts**
- **2 cups thawed COOL WHIP® Whipped Topping**

STIR pudding mix, pineapple with juice, marshmallows and nuts in large bowl until well blended. Gently stir in whipped topping.

REFRIGERATE 1 hour or until ready to serve. Garnish as desired.

Makes 8 servings

Peach Melba Dessert

Prep Time: 20 minutes   **Refrigerating Time:** 6 hours

1 ½ cups boiling water, divided
2 packages (4-serving size each) JELL-O® Brand Raspberry
    Flavor Sugar Free Low Calorie Gelatin Dessert or JELL-O®
    Brand Raspberry Flavor Gelatin Dessert, divided
1 container (8 ounces) BREYERS® Vanilla Lowfat Yogurt
1 cup raspberries, divided
1 can (8 ounces) peach slices in juice, undrained
    Cold water

STIR ¾ cup boiling water into 1 package of gelatin in large bowl at least 2 minutes or until completely dissolved. Refrigerate about 1 hour or until slightly thickened (consistency of unbeaten egg whites). Stir in yogurt and ½ cup raspberries. Reserve remaining raspberries for garnish. Pour gelatin mixture into serving bowl. Refrigerate about 2 hours or until set but not firm (gelatin should stick to finger when touched and should mound).

MEANWHILE, drain peaches, reserving juice. Add cold water to reserved juice to make 1 cup; set aside. Stir remaining ¾ cup boiling water into remaining package gelatin in large bowl at least 2 minutes until completely dissolved. Stir in measured juice and water. Refrigerate about 1 hour or until slightly thickened (consistency of unbeaten egg whites).

RESERVE several peach slices for garnish; chop remaining peaches. Stir chopped peaches into slightly thickened gelatin. Spoon over gelatin layer in bowl. Refrigerate 3 hours or until firm. Top with reserved peach slices and raspberries.   **Makes 8 servings**

Tropical Terrine

1 package (3 ounces) ladyfingers, split, divided
1½ cups boiling water
1 package (8-serving size) or 2 packages (4-serving size each)
    JELL-O® Brand Orange Flavor Sugar Free Low Calorie
    Gelatin Dessert
1 can (8 ounces) crushed pineapple in juice, undrained
1 cup cold water
2 cups thawed COOL WHIP LITE® Whipped Topping
1 can (11 ounces) mandarin orange segments, drained
    Additional thawed COOL WHIP LITE® Whipped Topping
    Kiwi slices
    Star fruit slices
    Pineapple leaves

LINE bottom and sides of 9×5-inch loaf pan with plastic wrap. Add enough ladyfingers, cut sides in, to fit evenly along all sides of pan.

STIR boiling water into gelatin in large bowl 2 minutes or until completely dissolved. Stir in pineapple with juice and cold water. Refrigerate 1¼ hours or until slightly thickened (consistency of unbeaten egg whites). Gently stir in 2 cups whipped topping and oranges. Spoon into prepared pan. Arrange remaining ladyfingers, cut sides down, evenly on top of gelatin mixture.

REFRIGERATE 3 hours or until firm. Place serving plate on top of pan. Invert, holding pan and plate together; shake gently to loosen. Carefully remove pan and plastic wrap. Garnish with additional whipped topping, fruit and pineapple leaves. **Makes 12 servings**

COOL TIP: If you put a dab of shortening in the corners of the loaf pan, the plastic wrap will adhere to the pan more smoothly and easily. To keep its shape, leftover dessert can be returned to the loaf pan and refrigerated.

Southern Banana Pudding

Prep Time: 30 minutes   **Bake Time:** 15 minutes

> 1 package (4-serving size) JELL-O® Vanilla or Banana Cream
>   Flavor Cook & Serve Pudding & Pie Filling (not Instant)
> 2½ cups milk
> 2 egg yolks, well beaten
> 30 to 35 vanilla wafers
> 2 large bananas, sliced
> 2 egg whites
>   Dash salt
> ¼ cup sugar

HEAT oven to 350°F.

STIR pudding mix into milk in medium saucepan. Add egg yolks. Stirring constantly, cook on medium heat until mixture comes to full boil. Remove from heat.

ARRANGE layer of cookies on bottom and up side of 1½-quart baking dish. Add layer of banana slices; top with ⅓ of the pudding. Repeat layers twice, ending with pudding.

BEAT egg whites and salt in medium bowl with electric mixer on high speed until foamy. Gradually add sugar, beating until stiff peaks form. Spoon meringue mixture lightly onto pudding, spreading to edge of dish to seal.

BAKE 10 to 15 minutes or until meringue is lightly browned. Serve warm or refrigerate until ready to serve.   **Makes 8 servings**

Waldorf Salad

Prep Time: 20 minutes   **Refrigerating Time:** 5½ hours

2 cups boiling water
1 package (8-serving size) or 2 packages (4-serving size each)
   JELL-O® Brand Lemon Flavor Gelatin Dessert
1 cup cold water
1 tablespoon lemon juice
½ cup KRAFT® Mayo: Real Mayonnaise or MIRACLE WHIP®
   Salad Dressing
1 medium red apple, diced
½ cup diced celery
¼ cup chopped walnuts
   Salad greens (optional)

STIR boiling water into gelatin in large bowl at least 2 minutes until completely dissolved. Stir in cold water and lemon juice. Refrigerate about 1½ hours or until thickened (spoon drawn through leaves definite impression). Gradually stir in mayonnaise with wire whisk. Stir in apple, celery and walnuts. Pour into 5-cup mold.

REFRIGERATE 4 hours or until firm. Unmold. Serve on salad greens, if desired.   **Makes 10 servings**

Easy Mallow Brulée

Prep Time: 10 minutes

2 cups cold half-and-half
1 package (4-serving size) JELL-O® Vanilla Flavor Instant
   Pudding & Pie Filling
1 cup JET-PUFFED® Miniature Marshmallows

POUR half-and-half into large bowl. Add pudding mix. Beat with wire whisk 2 minutes or until well blended. Pour into 4 (6-ounce) custard cups.

HEAT broiler. Top each cup with marshmallows. Broil about 6 to 8 inches from broiler, about 1 to 2 minutes or until marshmallows are golden brown, watching carefully.   **Makes 4 servings**

Great Substitute: Try using JELL-O® Lemon or Banana Flavor Instant Pudding instead of Vanilla Flavor.

Strawberry Lime Dessert

Prep Time: 15 minutes   **Refrigerating Time:** 3 hours

2 cups boiling water
1 package (4-serving size) JELL-O® Brand Lime Flavor Sugar
Free Low Calorie Gelatin Dessert or JELL-O® Brand Lime
Flavor Gelatin Dessert
½ cup cold water
1 container (8 ounces) BREYERS® Vanilla Lowfat Yogurt
1 package (4-serving size) JELL-O® Brand Strawberry Flavor
Sugar Free Low Calorie Gelatin Dessert or JELL-O® Brand
Strawberry Flavor Gelatin Dessert
1 package (10 ounces) frozen strawberries in lite syrup,
unthawed

STIR 1 cup of the boiling water into lime gelatin in medium bowl at least
2 minutes until completely dissolved. Stir in cold water. Refrigerate about
45 minutes or until slightly thickened (consistency of unbeaten egg whites).
Stir in yogurt with wire whisk until smooth. Pour into 2-quart serving bowl.
Refrigerate about 15 minutes or until set but not firm (gelatin should stick to
finger when touched and should mound).

STIR remaining 1 cup boiling water into strawberry gelatin in medium bowl
at least 2 minutes until completely dissolved. Stir in frozen berries until
berries are separated and gelatin is thickened (spoon drawn through leaves
definite impression). Spoon over lime gelatin mixture.

REFRIGERATE 2 hours or until firm. Garnish as desired.

Makes 10 servings

Tip

JELL-O® Fun Fact: The first JELL-O
flavors—strawberry, raspberry, orange
and lemon are still available today and
are among the most popular flavors.

Striped Delight

Prep Time: 20 minutes   **Refrigerating Time:** 4 hours 15 minutes

   35 **chocolate sandwich cookies, finely crushed (3 cups)**
    6 **tablespoons butter or margarine, melted**
    1 **package (8 ounces) PHILADELPHIA® Cream Cheese, softened**
  ¼ **cup sugar**
    2 **tablespoons cold milk**
    1 **tub (12 ounces) COOL WHIP® Whipped Topping, thawed**
 3¼ **cups cold milk**
    2 **packages (4-serving size each) JELL-O® Chocolate Flavor**
      Instant Pudding & Pie Filling

MIX crushed cookies and butter in medium bowl. Press firmly into bottom of foil-lined 13×9-inch pan. Refrigerate 15 minutes.

BEAT cream cheese, sugar and 2 tablespoons milk in medium bowl with wire whisk until smooth. Gently stir in 1¼ cups of the whipped topping. Spread over crust.

POUR 3¼ cups milk into large bowl. Add pudding mixes. Beat with wire whisk 1 to 2 minutes. Pour over cream cheese layer. Let stand 5 minutes or until thickened. Drop remaining whipped topping by spoonfuls over pudding. Spread to cover pudding.

REFRIGERATE 4 hours or overnight. Cut into squares.

Makes 16 servings

Tip: For easier cutting, place dessert in freezer 1 hour before serving.

Peanut Butter Loaf

Prep Time: 15 minutes   **Freeze Time:** 4 hours

> 1 package (16.1 ounces) JELL-O® No Bake Peanut Butter Cup
>   Dessert
> ⅓ cup butter or margarine, melted
> 1⅓ cups cold milk

PLACE topping pouch in large bowl of boiling water; set aside. Line 9×5-inch loaf pan with foil. Stir crust mix and butter with fork in medium bowl until crumbs are well moistened. Press ½ of crumbs firmly onto bottom of prepared pan; reserve remaining crumbs.

POUR cold milk into medium mixing bowl. Add filling mix and peanut butter. Beat with electric mixer on lowest speed until blended. Beat on high 3 minutes. Do not underbeat. Spoon ½ of filling mixture over crust in pan.

REMOVE pouch from water. Shake vigorously 60 seconds until topping is no longer lumpy. Squeeze ½ of topping over filling in pan. Repeat layers with remaining crumbs, filling and topping. Freeze 4 hours or overnight. To serve, lift from pan to cutting board and remove foil. Let stand at room temperature 10 minutes for easier slicing.   **Makes 8 to 10 servings**

Juiced Up Fruit Mold

Prep Time: 20 minutes   **Refrigerating Time:** 5½ hours

> 2½ cups boiling water
> 1 package (8-serving size) or 2 packages (4-serving size each)
>   JELL-O® Brand Gelatin, any red flavor
> 1 cup cold cranberry juice cocktail
> 1 can (11 ounces) mandarin orange segments, drained
> 1 cup halved seedless green grapes

STIR boiling water into gelatin in large bowl at least 2 minutes until completely dissolved. Stir in cold juice. Refrigerate about 1½ hours or until thickened (spoon drawn through leaves definite impression). Stir in fruit. Spoon into 6-cup mold which has been sprayed with no stick cooking spray.

REFRIGERATE about 4 hours or until firm. Unmold.

Makes 10 servings

Pastel Swirl Dessert

Prep Time: 30 minutes   **Refrigerating Time:** 4½ hours

> 1 package (3 ounces) ladyfingers, split
> 1⅓ cups boiling water
> 2 packages (4-serving size each) JELL-O® Brand Gelatin
>   Dessert, any 2 different flavors
> 1 cup cold water
>   Ice cubes
> 1 tub (12 ounces) COOL WHIP® Whipped Topping, thawed

TRIM about 1 inch off 1 end of each ladyfinger; reserve trimmed ends. Place ladyfingers, cut ends down, around side of 9-inch springform pan.* Place trimmed ends on bottom of pan.

STIR ⅔ cup of the boiling water into each package of gelatin in separate medium bowls at least 2 minutes until completely dissolved. Mix cold water and ice cubes to make 2½ cups. Stir ½ of the ice water into each bowl until gelatin is slightly thickened. Remove any remaining ice.

GENTLY stir ½ of the whipped topping with wire whisk into each gelatin mixture until smooth. Refrigerate 20 to 30 minutes or until mixtures are very thick and will mound. Spoon mixtures alternately into prepared pan. Swirl with knife to marbleize.

REFRIGERATE 4 hours or until firm. Remove side of pan.

Makes 16 servings

*To prepare in 13×9-inch pan, do not trim ladyfingers. Line bottom of pan with ladyfingers. Continue as directed.

Layered Orange Pineapple Mold

Prep Time: 20 minutes   **Refrigerating Time:** 6 hours

> **1 can (20 ounces) crushed pineapple in juice, undrained**
> **Cold water**
> **1½ cups boiling water**
> **1 package (8-serving size) or 2 packages (4-serving size each)**
> **JELL-O® Brand Orange Flavor Gelatin Dessert**
> **1 package (8 ounces) PHILADELPHIA® Cream Cheese, softened**

DRAIN pineapple, reserving juice. Add cold water to juice to make 1½ cups.

STIR boiling water into gelatin in large bowl at least 2 minutes until completely dissolved. Stir in measured pineapple juice and water. Reserve 1 cup gelatin at room temperature.

STIR ½ of the crushed pineapple into remaining gelatin. Pour into 6-cup mold. Refrigerate about 2 hours or until set but not firm (gelatin should stick to finger when touched and should mound).

STIR reserved 1 cup gelatin gradually into cream cheese in medium bowl with wire whisk until smooth. Stir in remaining crushed pineapple. Pour over gelatin layer in mold.

REFRIGERATE 4 hours or until firm. Unmold. Garnish as desired.

Makes 10 servings

To prevent drying, cover prepared gelatin before refrigerating to prevent drying.

Crown Jewel Dessert

Prep Time: 45 minutes   **Refrigerating Time:** 8¾ hours

- 1 package (4-serving size) JELL-O® Brand Lime Flavor Gelatin Dessert*
- 1 package (4-serving size) JELL-O® Brand Orange Flavor Gelatin Dessert*
- 1 package (4-serving size) JELL-O® Brand Strawberry Flavor Gelatin Dessert*
- 3 cups boiling water
- 1½ cups cold water
- 1 cup boiling water
- 1 package (4-serving size) JELL-O® Brand Strawberry Flavor Gelatin Dessert
- ½ cup cold water
- 1 tub (8 ounces) COOL WHIP® Whipped Topping, thawed

*Or use any 3 different flavors of JELL-O Brand Gelatin Dessert.

PREPARE lime, orange and 1 package strawberry gelatin separately as directed on packages, using 1 cup boiling water and ½ cup cold water for each. Pour each flavor into separate 8-inch square pans. Refrigerate 4 hours or until firm. Cut into ½-inch cubes; measure 1½ cups of each flavor. (Use the remaining gelatin cubes for garnish, if desired, or for snacking.)

STIR 1 cup boiling water into remaining package of strawberry gelatin in medium bowl at least 2 minutes until completely dissolved. Stir in ½ cup cold water. Refrigerate 45 minutes or until slightly thickened (consistency of unbeaten egg whites).

STIR in ½ of the whipped topping. Gently stir in measured gelatin cubes. Pour into 9×5-inch loaf pan.

REFRIGERATE 4 hours or until firm. Unmold. Garnish with remaining whipped topping and gelatin cubes, if desired.   **Makes 16 servings**

JELL-O®
BRAND

Snacks Aplenty

Creamy Cantaloupe

Prep Time: 15 minutes plus refrigerating

- **1 medium cantaloupe (about 3½ pounds)**
- **¾ cup boiling water**
- **1 package (4-serving size) JELL-O® Brand Gelatin, any flavor**
- **½ cup cold orange juice**
- **½ cup thawed COOL WHIP® Whipped Topping**

CUT melon in half lengthwise; remove seeds. Scoop out melon, leaving about 1-inch thick border of melon. Dice scooped out melon. Drain well. Cut thin slice from bottom of each melon shell to allow shells to stand upright, or place in small bowls.

STIR boiling water into gelatin in large bowl at least 2 minutes until completely dissolved. Stir in cold juice. Refrigerate 15 minutes or until slightly thickened (consistency of unbeaten egg whites). Gently stir in whipped topping. Stir in reserved diced melon. Pour into melon shells.

REFRIGERATE 3 hours or until firm. Cut into wedges.

Makes 8 servings

Super Cherry Cola Floats

Prep Time: 15 minutes plus refrigerating

1 cup boiling water
1 package (4-serving size) JELL-O® Brand Cherry Flavor Gelatin
1 ¼ cups cold cola
1 pint vanilla ice cream (2 cups)

STIR boiling water into gelatin in medium bowl 2 minutes until completely dissolved. Stir in cola. Refrigerate 20 to 30 minutes or until slightly thickened (consistency of unbeaten egg whites). Reserve ½ cup gelatin.

PLACE ½ cup ice cream into each of 4 tall ice cream soda glasses. Top with thickened gelatin mixture.

BEAT reserved ½ cup gelatin mixture with electric mixer on medium speed until light and fluffy. Spoon into each glass.

REFRIGERATE 2 hours or until firm.   **Makes 4 servings**

Special Extra: Garnish each float with a maraschino cherry and sprinkles.

Pudding Mix-Ins

Prep Time: 15 minutes   **Refrigerating Time:** 2 hours

2 cups cold milk
1 package (4-serving size) JELL-O® Instant Pudding & Pie
  Filling, any flavor
  Assorted "treasures": BAKER'S® Semi-Sweet Real Chocolate
    Chips, chopped nuts, miniature marshmallows, raisins,
    chopped bananas, halved grapes, crumbled chocolate
    sandwich cookies or peanut butter
Thawed COOL WHIP® Whipped Topping

POUR milk into medium bowl. Add pudding mix. Beat with wire whisk 2 minutes.

PLACE 1 tablespoon of the "treasures" into each of 4 dessert glasses. Spoon pudding over treasures.

REFRIGERATE until ready to serve. Top with whipped topping and garnish as desired.   **Makes 4 servings**

Super Cherry Cola Float

JELL-O® Glazed Popcorn

Prep Time: 10 minutes   **Cook Time:** 15 minutes

8 cups popped popcorn
1 cup salted peanuts or cashews
¼ cup butter or margarine
3 tablespoons light corn syrup
½ cup packed light brown sugar or granulated sugar
1 package (4-serving size) JELL-O® Brand Gelatin, any flavor

HEAT oven to 300°F. Line a 15×10×1-inch pan with foil or waxed paper. Place popcorn and nuts in large bowl.

HEAT butter and syrup in small saucepan over low heat. Stir in sugar and gelatin; bring to boil on medium heat. Reduce heat to low and gently simmer for 5 minutes. Immediately pour syrup over popcorn, tossing to coat well.

SPREAD popcorn in prepared pan, using two forks to spread evenly. Bake 10 minutes. Cool. Remove from pan and break into small pieces.

Makes about 9 cups

JELL-O® Jigglers® Snack Pops

Prep Time: 10 minutes plus refrigerating

1¼ cups boiling water
1 package (8-serving size) or 2 packages (4-serving size)
JELL-O® Brand Gelatin Dessert, any flavor
4 (5-ounce) paper cups
6 plastic straws, cut in half

STIR boiling water into gelatin in medium bowl at least 3 minutes until completely dissolved. Cool 15 minutes at room temperature. Pour into cups.

REFRIGERATE 3 hours or until firm. Carefully peel away cups. Using a knife dipped in warm water, cut each gelatin cup horizontally into 3 round slices. Insert straw into each gelatin slice to resemble a lollipop.

Makes 12 pops

Florida Sunshine Cups

Prep Time: 20 minutes plus refrigerating

> ¾ **cup boiling water**
> 1 **package (4-serving size) JELL-O® Brand Orange or Lemon**
>   **Flavor Sugar Free Low Calorie Gelatin**
> 1 **cup cold orange juice**
> ½ **cup fresh raspberries**
> 1 **can (11 ounces) mandarin orange segments, drained**

STIR boiling water into gelatin in large bowl at least 2 minutes until completely dissolved. Stir in cold juice. Refrigerate 1½ hours or until thickened (spoon drawn through leaves definite impression).

MEASURE ¾ cup thickened gelatin into medium bowl; set aside. Stir fruit into remaining gelatin. Pour into serving bowl or 6 dessert dishes.

BEAT reserved gelatin with electric mixer on high speed until fluffy and about doubled in volume. Spoon over gelatin in bowl or dishes.

REFRIGERATE 3 hours or until firm.   **Makes 6 servings**

Cherry Pie Squares

Prep Time: 10 minutes

> 1 **package (12 ounces) pound cake, cut into 10 slices**
> 1 **can (21 ounces) cherry pie filling**
> 2¼ **cups cold milk**
> 2 **packages (4-serving size each) JELL-O® Vanilla or Lemon**
>   **Flavor Instant Pudding & Pie Filling**
> 1 **tub (8 ounces) COOL WHIP® Whipped Topping, thawed**

ARRANGE cake slices in bottom of 9×13-inch baking pan. Top with pie filling.

POUR milk into large bowl. Add pudding mixes. Beat with wire whisk 2 minutes or until well blended. Gently stir in 1 cup of the whipped topping. Spoon mixture over pie filling in pan. Top with remaining whipped topping.

REFRIGERATE until ready to serve or overnight. Garnish as desired.
                    Makes 15 servings

Make-Ahead: This recipe is great for a crowd and is even better when prepared the night before!

Applesauce Yogurt Delight

Prep Time: 15 minutes plus refrigerating

　　1 cup boiling water
　　1 package (4-serving size) JELL-O® Brand Gelatin, any red
　　　　flavor
　　¾ cup cold applesauce
　　¼ teaspoon ground cinnamon
　　½ cup BREYERS® Vanilla Lowfat Yogurt

STIR boiling water into gelatin in medium bowl at least 2 minutes until completely dissolved. Measure ¾ cup; stir in applesauce and cinnamon. Pour into bowl or 4 dessert dishes. Refrigerate about 15 minutes or until set but not firm.

REFRIGERATE remaining gelatin until slightly thickened (consistency of unbeaten egg whites). Mix in yogurt; spoon over gelatin in bowl.

REFRIGERATE 2 hours or until set.　　　　　　**Makes 4 servings**

Variation: This recipe can be made with JELL-O® Brand Sugar Free Low Calorie Gelatin with superb results!

Pudding Café

Prep Time: 5 minutes　　**Refrigerating Time:** 2 hours

　　2 cups cold milk
　　1 package (4-serving size) JELL-O® Chocolate or Vanilla Flavor
　　　　Instant Pudding & Pie Filling
　　¼ cup GENERAL FOODS INTERNATIONAL COFFEES®, any
　　　　flavor

POUR milk into medium bowl. Add pudding mix and flavored instant coffee. Beat with wire whisk 2 minutes. Refrigerate until ready to serve.

Makes 4 servings

Creamy Tropical Island Squares

Prep Time: 15 minutes plus refrigerating

> **2 cups** finely crushed NABISCO® Old Fashioned Ginger Snaps
> **¼ cup** sugar
> **⅓ cup** butter or margarine, melted
> **1½ cups** boiling water
> **1 package** (8-serving size) or **2 packages** (4-serving size each)
>   JELL-O® Brand Lemon Flavor Gelatin
> **1 can** (20 ounces) crushed pineapple in juice
>   Cold water
> **1 package** (8 ounces) PHILADELPHIA® Cream Cheese, softened
> **1 tub** (8 ounces) COOL WHIP® Whipped Topping, thawed
> **1 cup** chopped strawberries
> **1 cup** toasted BAKER'S® ANGEL FLAKE® Coconut (optional)

MIX ginger snap crumbs, sugar and butter in 13×9-inch baking pan until crumbs are well moistened. Press firmly onto bottom of pan. Refrigerate until ready to fill.

STIR boiling water into gelatin in large bowl at least 2 minutes until completely dissolved. Drain pineapple, reserving juice. Set aside pineapple. Mix juice and water to make 2 cups. Stir into gelatin. Whisk in cream cheese until well blended. Refrigerate about 1½ hours or until thickened (spoon drawn through leaves definite impression).

STIR whipped topping into gelatin mixture with wire whisk until smooth. Pour mixture over crust.

REFRIGERATE 3 hours or until firm. Top with pineapple and strawberries. Sprinkle with coconut.   **Makes 15 servings**

Helpful Hint: Soften cream cheese in microwave on HIGH 15 to 20 seconds.

Great Substitute: Try JELL-O® Brand Orange Flavor Gelatin instead of Lemon Flavor.

Hidden Treasure Macaroons

Prep Time: 10 minutes   **Bake Time:** 20 minutes

¾ cup cold milk
1 teaspoon vanilla
1 package (4-serving size) JELL-O® Vanilla Flavor Instant Pudding & Pie Filling
1 package (14 ounces) BAKER'S® ANGEL FLAKE® Coconut
¼ cup all-purpose flour
BAKER'S® Semi-Sweet Chocolate Chunks

HEAT oven to 350°F.

POUR milk and vanilla into medium bowl. Add pudding mix. Beat with wire whisk 1 minute or until smooth. Add coconut and flour. Stir to combine completely. Mixture will be stiff. With hands, roll cookie dough into balls, about 1 inch in diameter. Insert chocolate chunk into center of each ball, closing up the end to cover chocolate. Place balls 1 inch apart on lightly greased and floured cookie sheets.

BAKE 15 to 20 minutes or until edges of cookies are golden brown. Immediately remove from cookie sheets. Cool on wire racks.

Makes about 3 dozen cookies

Black and White Hidden Treasures: Prepare Macaroons as directed above, substituting JELL-O® Chocolate Flavor Instant Pudding & Pie Filling for vanilla flavor and BAKER'S® Premium White Chocolate Chunks for semi-sweet chocolate chunks.

Nutty Banana Treasures: Prepare Macaroons as directed above substituting JELL-O® Banana Cream Flavor Instant Pudding & Pie filling for vanilla flavor and pecans or walnuts for chocolate chunks.

Thumbprint Macaroons: Prepare Macaroons and form into balls as directed above. Place 1 inch apart on greased and floured cookie sheets. Press each ball with thumb to create a depression in the center of dough. Place chocolate chunk in the center of each cookie. Bake as directed above.

Chewy Fruit & Nut Bars

Prep Time: 15 minutes plus refrigerating

> **2 cups LORNA DOONE® Shortbread crumbs**
> **5 tablespoons butter or margarine, melted**
> **1 cup boiling water**
> **2 packages (4-serving size each) JELL-O® Brand Apricot or Peach Flavor Gelatin**
> **½ cup light corn syrup**
> **1 cup chopped toasted PLANTERS® Slivered Almonds**

STIR crumbs and butter in 9-inch square baking pan until crumbs are well moistened, reserving ½ cup crumb mixture. Firmly press remaining crumbs onto bottom of pan. Refrigerate until ready to fill.

STIR boiling water into gelatin in large bowl at least 2 minutes until completely dissolved. Stir in corn syrup. Refrigerate 15 minutes or until slightly thickened (consistency of unbeaten egg whites). Stir in almonds. Pour into pan over crust. Sprinkle with remaining crumbs.

REFRIGERATE 3 hours or until firm. Cut into bars.   **Makes 20 bars**

Great Substitute: Use JELL-O® Brand Orange Flavor Gelatin instead of Apricot Flavor. Reduce almonds to ½ cup and add ½ cup chopped dried apricots.

Snacks Aplenty

Easy 5-Minute Desserts

Warm Cinnamon Bun Pudding: Prepare 1 package (4-serving size) Vanilla Flavor JELL-O® Instant Pudding as directed on package. Stir in ½ teaspoon ground cinnamon. Spoon into microwavable dessert dishes. Swirl 1 tablespoon caramel dessert topping into each serving. Microwave each serving (½ cup) on HIGH 35 seconds or until pudding is heated through. Top each with a dollop of thawed COOL WHIP® Whipped Topping and sprinkle with chopped toasted PLANTERS® Pecan Pieces. Stir and serve immediately. Makes 4 servings

Eggnog Custard Cups: Prepare 1 package (4-serving size) Vanilla Flavor JELL-O® Instant Pudding as directed on package substituting half-and-half for the milk. Stir in ¼ teaspoon ground nutmeg and ½ teaspoon rum extract. Spoon into individual dessert dishes. Top each with a dollop of thawed COOL WHIP® Whipped Topping and sprinkle with additional nutmeg, if desired. Makes 4 servings

Mocha Cups: Prepare 1 package (4-serving size) Chocolate Flavor JELL-O® Instant Pudding as directed on package. Stir in 2 teaspoons instant espresso powder. Gently stir in 1 cup thawed COOL WHIP® Whipped Topping. Spoon into individual dessert dishes. Top each with a dollop of thawed COOL WHIP® Whipped Topping and sprinkle with ground cinnamon, if desired. Makes 4 servings

"No Pumpkin" Pie Cups: Prepare 1 package (4-serving size) Vanilla Flavor JELL-O® Instant Pudding as directed on package. Stir in 1 teaspoon pumpkin pie spice and 1 cup chopped NABISCO® Old Fashioned Ginger Snaps. Spoon into individual dessert dishes. Top each with a dollop of thawed COOL WHIP® Whipped Topping, if desired. Makes 4 servings

Easy Lemon Pudding Cookies

Prep Time: 10 minutes   **Bake Time:** 10 minutes

> **1 cup BISQUICK® Original Baking Mix**
> **1 package (4-serving size) JELL-O® Lemon Flavor Instant**
>   **Pudding & Pie Filling**
> **½ teaspoon ground ginger (optional)**
> **1 egg, lightly beaten**
> **¼ cup vegetable oil**
>   **Sugar**
> **3 squares BAKER'S® Premium White Baking Chocolate, melted**

HEAT oven to 350°F.

STIR baking mix, pudding mix and ginger in medium bowl. Mix in egg and oil until well blended. (Mixture will be stiff.) With hands, roll cookie dough into 1-inch diameter balls. Place balls 2 inches apart on lightly greased cookie sheets. Dip flat-bottom glass into sugar. Press glass onto each dough ball and flatten into ¼-inch-thick cookie.

BAKE 10 minutes or until edges are golden brown. Immediately remove from cookie sheets. Cool on wire racks. Drizzle cookies with melted white chocolate.   **Makes about 20 cookies**

How To Melt Chocolate: Microwave 3 squares BAKER'S® Premium White Baking Chocolate in heavy zipper-style plastic sandwich bag on HIGH 1 to 1½ minutes or until chocolate is almost melted. Gently knead bag until chocolate is completely melted. Fold down top of bag; snip tiny piece off 1 corner from bottom. Holding top of bag tightly, drizzle chocolate through opening across tops of cookies.

JELL-O® Frozen No Bake Peanut Butter Cups

Prep Time: 15 minutes plus freezing

    1 package (16.1 ounces) JELL-O® No Bake Peanut Butter Cup Dessert
    ⅓ cup melted margarine
    1⅓ cups cold milk

PLACE topping pouch in large bowl of boiling water; set aside.

PREPARE crust mix as directed on package in medium bowl. Press onto bottoms of 12 to 15 foil-cup-lined muffin cups (about 1 heaping tablespoon per muffin cup).

PREPARE filling mix as directed on package in deep, medium bowl. Divide filling among muffin cups. Remove pouch from water; knead pouch 60 seconds until fluid and no longer lumpy. Squeeze topping equally over cups.

FREEZE 2 hours or until firm. Store, covered, in freezer up to 2 weeks.

Makes 12 to 15 cups

JELL-O® Frozen No Bake Cookies & Creme Cups: Prepare JELL-O® No Bake Cookies & Creme Dessert as directed on package, pressing prepared crust mix onto bottoms of 12 foil-cup-lined muffin cups. Divide prepared filling mixture among cups. Top with reserved cookies. Freeze and store as directed above.

Tip

Cold and smooth, this snack is the perfect hot-weather treat when you don't want to heat up your oven.

Fruited Snack Cups

Prep Time: 20 minutes plus refrigerating

> ¾ **cup boiling water**
> 1 **package (4-serving size) JELL-O® Brand Strawberry Flavor**
>   **Gelatin, or any red flavor**
> 1 **cup cold orange juice**
>   **Ice cubes**
> ¾ **cup thawed COOL WHIP® Whipped Topping**
> 1 **can (11 ounces) mandarin orange segments, drained**

STIR boiling water into gelatin in large bowl at least 2 minutes until completely dissolved. Mix cold juice and ice cubes to make 1¼ cups. Add to gelatin, stirring until slightly thickened (consistency of unbeaten egg whites). Remove any remaining ice.

MEASURE 1 cup gelatin and stir in whipped topping with wire whisk until smooth. Pour about 2 tablespoons into each of 12 paper or foil-lined muffin cups. Refrigerate about 25 minutes or until set but not firm (should stick to finger when touched and should mound). Stir fruit into remaining gelatin and carefully spoon over creamy layer, dividing evenly among muffin cups.

REFRIGERATE 3 hours or until firm.   **Makes 12 servings**

Tip: This recipe can be made in a plastic container with a cover for a great take-along school snack!

Strawberry Banana Smoothie

Prep Time: 5 minutes

> 2 **cups crushed ice**
> 1 **cup cold milk**
> 1 **package (4-serving size) JELL-O® Brand Strawberry Flavor**
>   **Gelatin Dessert**
> 1 **container (8 ounces) BREYERS® Vanilla Lowfat Yogurt**
> 1 **large banana, cut into chunks**

PLACE all ingredients in blender container; cover. Blend on high speed 30 seconds or until smooth. Serve immediately.   **Makes 4 servings**

Yogurt Fluff

Prep Time: 10 minutes plus refrigerating

> ¾ **cup boiling water**
> 1 **package (4-serving size) JELL-O® Brand Sugar Free Low Calorie Gelatin Dessert or JELL-O® Brand Gelatin Dessert, any flavor**
> ½ **cup cold water or fruit juice**
>   **Ice cubes**
> 1 **container (8 ounces) BREYERS® Vanilla Lowfat Yogurt**
> ½ **teaspoon vanilla (optional)**
> 5 **tablespoons thawed COOL WHIP FREE® or COOL WHIP LITE® Whipped Topping**

STIR boiling water into gelatin in large bowl at least 2 minutes until completely dissolved.

MIX cold water and ice cubes to make 1 cup. Add to gelatin, stirring until slightly thickened. Remove any remaining ice. Stir in yogurt and vanilla. Pour into dessert dishes.

REFRIGERATE 1½ hours or until firm. Top with whipped topping.

Makes 5 servings

Chocolaty-Rich Hot Cocoa

Prep Time: 10 minutes

> 1 **package (4-serving size) JELL-O® Chocolate Flavor Cook & Serve Pudding & Pie Filling (not Instant)**
> 1½ **quarts milk**
> ½ **cup BAKER'S® Semi-Sweet Chocolate Chunks**
> ½ **teaspoon vanilla**
>   **Thawed COOL WHIP® Whipped Topping or JET-PUFFED® Miniature Marshmallows (optional)**

STIR pudding mix and milk in medium saucepan with wire whisk until blended. Stirring constantly, cook over medium heat until mixture comes to full boil. Remove from heat. Add chocolate chunks and vanilla. Stir with wire whisk until well blended.

POUR into mugs and garnish with a dollop of whipped topping or several marshmallows. Serve immediately.

Makes 6 servings

Juicy JELL-O®

Prep Time: 5 minutes plus refrigerating

1 cup boiling water
1 package (4-serving size) JELL-O® Brand Gelatin, any flavor
1 cup cold juice, any flavor

STIR boiling water into gelatin in medium bowl at least 2 minutes until completely dissolved. Stir in cold juice.

REFRIGERATE 4 hours or until firm.   **Makes 4 (½-cup) servings**

Note: Do not use fresh or frozen pineapple, kiwi, papaya or guava juice. Gelatin will not set.

Variation: For fruited Juicy JELL-O®, prepare as directed but refrigerate for just 30 minutes until slightly thickened. Stir in 1 cup raspberries, blueberries or chopped strawberries. Refrigerate 4 hours or until firm.

Pudding in a Cloud

Prep Time: 15 minutes   **Refrigerating Time:** 2 hours

2 cups COOL WHIP® Whipped Topping, thawed
2 cups cold milk
1 package (4-serving size) JELL-O® Instant Pudding & Pie
    Filling, any flavor

SPOON whipped topping evenly into 6 dessert dishes. Using back of spoon, make depression in center; spread whipped topping up side of each dish.

POUR milk into medium bowl. Add pudding mix. Beat with wire whisk 2 minutes. Let stand 5 minutes. Spoon pudding into center of whipped topping.

REFRIGERATE until ready to serve.   **Makes 6 servings**

Lemon Bars

Prep Time: 10 minutes   **Refrigerate Time:** 4 hours

    15 whole graham crackers
     2 packages (8 ounces each) PHILADELPHIA® Cream Cheese,
        softened
  3½ cups cold milk
     3 packages (4-serving size each) JELL-O® Lemon Flavor Instant
        Pudding & Pie Filling
     1 tub (8 ounces) COOL WHIP® Whipped Topping, thawed,
        divided

ARRANGE ½ of the crackers in bottom of 13×9-inch pan, cutting crackers to fit, if necessary.

BEAT cream cheese in large bowl with electric mixer on low speed until smooth. Gradually beat in 1 cup of the milk. Add remaining milk and pudding mixes. Beat 1 to 2 minutes. (Mixture will be thick.) Gently stir in 2 cups of the whipped topping.

SPREAD ½ of the pudding mixture over crackers in pan. Arrange remaining crackers over pudding in pan. Top with remaining pudding mixture. Cover with remaining whipped topping. Refrigerate 4 hours or freeze 3 hours. Cut into bars.   **Makes 18 servings**

Tip

Garnish with fresh seasonal berries,
if desired.

Fruit Whip

Prep Time: 10 minutes plus refrigerating

> ¾ **cup boiling water**
> 1 **package (4-serving size) JELL-O® Brand Orange Flavor Gelatin**
> ½ **cup cold orange juice**
>   **Ice cubes**
> 1 **can (11 ounces) mandarin orange segments, drained (optional)**

STIR boiling water into gelatin in large bowl at least 2 minutes until completely dissolved. Mix cold juice and ice cubes to make 1¼ cups. Add to gelatin, stirring until ice cubes are partially melted. Place in blender container; cover. Blend on medium speed 15 seconds. Pour into 6 dessert glasses or large glass serving bowl. Spoon in fruit.

REFRIGERATE 25 minutes or until set. The mixture sets with frothy layer on top and clear layer on bottom.   **Makes 6 servings**

Great Substitute: Prepare as directed above, using any red flavor JELL-O® Brand Gelatin and apple or cranberry juice.

Refreshers

Prep Time: 5 minutes plus refrigerating

> 1 **cup boiling water**
> 1 **package (4-serving size) JELL-O® Brand Gelatin Dessert, any flavor**
> 1 **cup cold beverage, such as seltzer, club soda, ginger ale, iced tea or lemon-lime carbonated beverage**

STIR boiling water into gelatin in medium bowl at least 2 minutes until completely dissolved. Stir in cold beverage.

REFRIGERATE 4 hours or until firm. Cut into cubes and garnish as desired.
                Makes 4 servings

Sugar Free Low Calorie Refreshers: Prepare recipe as directed above using any flavor JELL-O® Brand Sugar Free Low Calorie Gelatin Dessert and 1 cup seltzer, club soda, diet ginger ale, diet iced tea or diet lemon-lime carbonated beverage.

Snacks Aplenty

Easy Pudding Milk Shake

Prep Time: 5 minutes

> 3 cups cold milk
> 1 package (4-serving size) JELL-O® Instant Pudding & Pie
>   Filling, any flavor
> 1½ cups ice cream, any flavor

POUR milk into blender container. Add pudding mix and ice cream; cover. Blend on high speed 30 seconds or until smooth. Pour into glasses and garnish as desired. Serve immediately.   **Makes 5 servings**

Citrus Coconut Squares

Prep Time: 15 minutes plus refrigerating

> 2 cups LORNA DOONE® Shortbread crumbs
> ¼ cup sugar
> ⅓ cup butter or margarine, melted
> ⅔ cup boiling orange juice
> 1 package (4-serving size) Orange or Lemon Flavor JELL-O®
>   Brand Gelatin
> ½ cup cold orange juice
>   Ice cubes
> 1 tub (12 ounces) COOL WHIP® Whipped Topping, thawed,
>   divided
> ½ cup BAKER'S® ANGEL FLAKE® Coconut, toasted

MIX crumbs, sugar and butter with fork in 13×9-inch baking pan until crumbs are well moistened. Press firmly onto bottom of pan. Refrigerate until ready to fill.

STIR boiling juice into gelatin in large bowl at least 2 minutes until completely dissolved. Mix cold juice and ice cubes to make 1¼ cups. Add to gelatin, stirring until slightly thickened (consistency of unbeaten egg whites). Remove any remaining ice. Stir in 3½ cups of the whipped topping with wire whisk until smooth. Pour over crust.

REFRIGERATE 3 hours or until firm. Just before serving, spread remaining whipped topping over gelatin mixture. Sprinkle coconut on top. Cut into squares.   **Makes 15 to 18 servings**

Hint: For a great twist, add 1 cup of seasonal berries to the thickened gelatin and proceed as directed.

JELL-O®
BRAND

Fun-Filled Favorites

Magical Marshmallow Carpets

Prep Time: 10 minutes   **Refrigerating Time:** 1 hour

1 package (8-serving size) or 2 packages (4-serving size each) JELL-O® Brand Gelatin Dessert, any flavor
1 cup warm water
3 cups JET-PUFFED® Miniature Marshmallows or 12 JET-PUFFED® Marshmallows

LIGHTLY GREASE 13×9-inch baking pan with no stick cooking spray.

STIR gelatin and water in medium microwavable bowl. Microwave on HIGH 2½ minutes; stir until dissolved.

STIR in marshmallows. Microwave on HIGH 2 minutes or until marshmallows are partially melted. Stir mixture slowly until marshmallows are completely melted. Pour mixture into pan.

REFRIGERATE 1 hour or until set. Cut gelatin into 2¼×4¼-inch rectangles. With marshmallow layer on top, cut small slits on each side of the rectangles to form "carpet fringe." Garnish each "carpet" with multicolored sprinkles, if desired.   **Makes 16 pieces**

Fun-Filled Favorites

Creamy Orange Cookie Cups

Prep Time: 5 minutes   **Refrigerating Time:** 2 hours

> 1¼ cups boiling water
> 1 package (4-serving size) JELL-O® Brand Orange Flavor
>   Gelatin Dessert
> 1 pint vanilla ice cream (2 cups)
> 16 NILLA® Wafers, divided

STIR boiling water into gelatin in medium bowl at least 2 minutes until completely dissolved. Stir in ice cream until melted. Place 1 cookie into each of 8 small cups. Pour gelatin into cups.

REFRIGERATE 2 hours or until firm. Garnish with remaining cookies and thawed COOL WHIP® Whipped Topping, if desired.   **Makes 8 servings**

Great Substitute: Try NILLA® Chocolate Wafers instead of the NILLA® Wafers.

Aquarium Cups

Prep Time: 10 minutes   **Refrigerating Time:** 1 hour

> ¾ cup boiling water
> 1 package (4-serving size) JELL-O® Brand Berry Blue Flavor
>   Gelatin Dessert
> ½ cup cold water
>   Ice cubes
>   Gummy fish

POUR boiling water into gelatin in medium bowl at least 2 minutes until completely dissolved. Mix cold water and ice cubes to make 1¼ cups. Add to gelatin, stirring until slightly thickened. Remove any remaining ice. (If mixture is still thin, refrigerate until slightly thickened.)

CUT thickened gelatin into 4 dessert dishes. Suspend gummy fish in gelatin. Refrigerate 1 hour or until firm.   **Makes 4 servings**

Fun-Filled Favorites

Pudding Chillers

Prep Time: 10 minutes   **Freeze Time:** 5 hours

2 cups cold milk
1 package (4-serving size) JELL-O® Instant Pudding & Pie
    Filling, any flavor
6 (5-ounce) paper cups

POUR milk into medium bowl. Add pudding mix. Beat with wire whisk
2 minutes. Spoon into cups. Insert wooden pop stick into each for a handle.

FREEZE 5 hours or overnight until firm. To remove pop from cup, place
bottom of cup under warm running water for 15 seconds. Press firmly on
bottom of cup to release pop. (Do not twist or pull pop stick.)

Makes 6 pops

Rocky Road: Use JELL-O® Chocolate Flavor Instant Pudding & Pie Filling
and stir in ½ cup miniature marshmallows and ¼ cup each BAKER'S®
Semi-Sweet Real Chocolate Chips and chopped peanuts.

Toffee Crunch: Use JELL-O® Vanilla Flavor Instant Pudding & Pie Filling and
stir in ½ cup chopped chocolate-covered toffee bars.

Cookies & Cream: Use JELL-O® Vanilla Flavor Instant Pudding & Pie Filling
and stir in ½ cup chopped chocolate sandwich cookies.

JELL-O® Jigglers®

Prep Time: 10 minutes   **Refrigerating Time:** 3 hours

2½ cups boiling juice (Do not add cold water)
2 packages (8-serving size each) or 4 packages (4-serving size
    each) JELL-O® Brand Gelatin Dessert, any flavor

STIR boiling juice into gelatin in large bowl at least 3 minutes until
completely dissolved. Pour into 13×9-inch pan.

REFRIGERATE 3 hours or until firm (does not stick to finger when
touched). Dip bottom of pan in warm water about 15 seconds. Cut into
decorative shapes with cookie cutters all the way through gelatin or cut into
1-inch squares. Lift from pan.   **Makes about 24 pieces**

Note: Recipe can be halved. Use 8- or 9-inch square pan.

*Clockwise from top left: **Rocky Road Pudding Chillers, Cookies & Cream Pudding Chillers,
Pudding in a Cloud** (page 86), **JELL-O® Jigglers®** and **Creamy JELL-O® JIGGLERS®** (page 98)*

Fun-Filled Favorites

Creamy JELL-O® Jigglers®

Prep Time: 15 minutes   **Refrigerating Time:** 3 hours

2½ cups boiling water
2 packages (8-serving size each) or 4 packages (4-serving size
each) JELL-O® Brand Gelatin Dessert, any flavor
1 cup cold milk
1 package (4-serving size) JELL-O® Vanilla Flavor Instant
Pudding & Pie Filling

STIR boiling water into gelatin in large bowl at least 3 minutes until completely dissolved. Cool 30 minutes at room temperature.

POUR milk into medium bowl. Add pudding mix. Beat with wire whisk 1 minute. Quickly pour into gelatin. Stir with wire whisk until well blended. Pour into 13×9-inch pan.

REFRIGERATE 3 hours or until firm. Dip bottom of pan in warm water about 15 seconds. Cut into decorative shapes with cookie cutters all the way through gelatin or cut into 1-inch squares. Lift from pan.

Makes about 24 pieces

Cosmic Clouds

Prep Time: 15 minutes   **Refrigerating Time:** 3 hours

1 tub (8 ounces) COOL WHIP® Whipped Topping, thawed
1½ cups boiling water
1 package (8-serving size) or 2 packages (4-serving size each)
JELL-O® Brand Gelatin Dessert, any flavor
1 can (15.25 ounces) pineapple cosmic fun shapes, drained,
reserving juice
Ice cubes

SPOON about ⅓ cup of the whipped topping into each of 10 dessert dishes. Using back of spoon, spread whipped topping into bottom and up side of each dish. Refrigerate until ready to fill.

STIR boiling water into gelatin in large bowl at least 2 minutes until completely dissolved. Mix reserved juice and enough ice cubes to make 2 cups. Add to gelatin, stirring until slightly thickened (consistency of unbeaten egg whites). If necessary, refrigerate to thicken gelatin. Stir in pineapple fun shapes. Fill center of whipped topping with gelatin mixture.

REFRIGERATE 3 hours or until firm.   **Makes 10 servings**

Frozen NUTTER BUTTER®
Peanut Butter Dessert

Prep Time: 15 minutes   **Freeze Time:** 2 hours

>   1 package (16.1 ounces) JELL-O® No Bake Peanut Butter Cup
>   Dessert
>   6 tablespoons butter or margarine, melted
>   1 package (16 ounces) NUTTER BUTTER® Peanut Butter
>   Sandwich Cookies, divided
> 1 ⅓ cups cold milk
>   1 tub (8 ounces) COOL WHIP® Whipped Topping, thawed

PLACE Topping Pouch in large bowl of boiling water; set aside.

LINE 8-inch square baking pan with foil extending over edges to form handles.

STIR Crust Mix and butter thoroughly in medium bowl until crumbs are well moistened. Firmly press crumbs onto bottom of pan, using small measuring cup. Using approximately 20 sandwich cookies, line sides of pan with cookies in upright position. Chop or crush remaining cookies into small bite-size pieces. Set aside.

POUR milk into medium bowl. Add Filling Mix and Peanut Butter. Beat with electric mixer on lowest speed 30 seconds. Beat on highest speed 3 minutes. DO NOT UNDERBEAT. (Filling will be thick.) Gently stir whipped topping into peanut butter mixture until completely mixed. Gently stir in reserved cookie pieces. Carefully spoon mixture into pan. Smooth top with spatula.

REMOVE pouch from water. Knead pouch 60 seconds until fluid and no longer lumpy. Pour topping over filling. Tilt pan to evenly cover filling. (Topping will harden during freezing.)

FREEZE 2 hours or until firm. To serve, lift from pan, using foil as handles, onto cutting board. Remove foil. Cut into squares.   **Makes 8 servings**

Frozen NUTTER BUTTER® Peanut Butter Pops: Prepare crust as directed above, pressing crumbs onto bottoms of 12 paper-lined muffin cups. Prepare filling as directed above omitting whipped topping and chopped cookies. Divide mixture among cups. Prepare topping as directed above and drizzle over each cup. Press 1 NUTTER BUTTER® Peanut Butter Sandwich Cookie halfway into each cup to serve as handle. Freeze 2 hours or until firm.

Fun-Filled Favorites

Dirt Cups

Prep Time: 15 minutes   **Refrigerating Time:** 2 hours

1 package (16 ounces) chocolate sandwich cookies
2 cups cold milk
1 package (4-serving size) JELL-O® Chocolate Flavor Instant
   Pudding & Pie Filling
1 tub (8 ounces) COOL WHIP® Whipped Topping, thawed
8 to 10 (7-ounce) paper or plastic cups
   Suggested garnishes: gummy worms or other gummy
      candies, candy flowers, chopped peanuts, granola

CRUSH cookies in zipper-style plastic bag with rolling pin or in food processor.

POUR milk into large bowl. Add pudding mix. Beat with wire whisk 2 minutes. Stir in whipped topping and ½ of the crushed cookies.

PLACE about 1 tablespoon of the crushed cookies in each cup. Fill cups about ¾ full with pudding mixture. Top with remaining crushed cookies.

REFRIGERATE until ready to serve. Garnish as desired.

Makes 8 to 10 servings

Tip

For Sand Cups, use 1 package
(12 ounces) vanilla wafer cookies and
JELL-O® Vanilla Flavor Instant
Pudding & Pie Filling.

Left to right: **Sand Cups** and **Dirt Cups**

Fruity Gelatin Pops

Prep: 10 minutes   **Freeze Time:** 7 hours

> **1 cup boiling water**
> **1 package (4-serving size) JELL-O® Brand Gelatin Dessert, any flavor**
> **⅓ cup sugar**
> **1 ⅓ cups cold juice, any flavor**
> **6 (5-ounce) paper cups**

STIR boiling water into gelatin and sugar in medium bowl at least 2 minutes until completely dissolved. Stir in cold juice. Pour into cups. Freeze about 2 hours or until almost firm. Insert wooden pop stick into each for handle.

FREEZE 5 hours or overnight until firm. To remove pop from cup, place bottom of cup under warm running water for 15 seconds. Press firmly on bottom of cup to release pop. (Do not twist or pull pop stick.) Store leftover pops in freezer up to 2 weeks.   **Makes 6 pops**

Outrageous Orange Pops: Use 1 cup boiling water, JELL-O® Brand Orange Flavor Gelatin Dessert, ⅓ cup sugar and 1 ⅓ cups orange juice.

Fruity Strawberry Pops: Use 1 cup boiling water, JELL-O® Brand Strawberry Flavor Gelatin Dessert, ⅓ cup sugar, ⅔ cup cold water and ⅔ cup puréed strawberries.

Fizzy Grape Pops: Use 1 cup boiling water, JELL-O® Brand Sparkling White Grape Flavor Gelatin Dessert, 2 tablespoons sugar and 1 ½ cups carbonated grape beverage.

Lemonade Pops: Use 1 cup boiling water, JELL-O® Brand Lemon Flavor Gelatin Dessert, ⅓ cup sugar, 1 cup cold water and 2 tablespoons lemon juice.

Iced Tea Pops: Use 1 cup boiling water, JELL-O® Brand Lemon Flavor Gelatin Dessert, 2 tablespoons sugar and 1 ½ cups pre-sweetened iced tea.

Top to bottom: **Lemonade Pops** and **Outrageous Orange Pops**

Fun-Filled Favorites

Monkey Shake

Prep Time: 10 minutes

> 2 cups cold milk
> 1 ripe banana
> 1 package (4-serving size) JELL-O® Chocolate Flavor Instant
>   Pudding & Pie Filling
> 2 cups crushed ice

POUR milk into blender container. Add banana, pudding mix and ice; cover. Blend on high speed 15 seconds or until smooth. Serve at once.

Makes 4 servings

How To: Mixture will thicken as it stands. To thin, just add more milk, ¼ cup at a time for desired thickness.

Great Substitute: Try using JELL-O® White Chocolate Flavor Instant Pudding & Pie Filling instead of Chocolate Flavor.

Key Lime Smoothie

Prep Time: 10 minutes

> ½ cup boiling water
> 1 package (4-serving size) JELL-O® Brand Lime Flavor Gelatin
>   Dessert
> 1 cup ice cubes
>   Cold water
> 1 ½ cups thawed COOL WHIP® Whipped Topping

STIR boiling water into gelatin in medium bowl at least 2 minutes until completely dissolved. Mix ice and enough cold water to make 1 ½ cups.

POUR gelatin, ice water and whipped topping into blender container; cover. Blend on medium speed until smooth. Serve immediately.

Makes 4 servings

Special Extras: Garnish each smoothie with a fresh whole strawberry and a large dollop of thawed COOL WHIP® Whipped Topping.

Great Substitute: Try any flavor JELL-O® Brand Gelatin Dessert for a delicious treat!

Left to Right: **Key Lime Smoothie** and **Monkey Shake**

JELL-O®
BRAND

Luscious Layers

Chocolate Passion Layered Dessert

Prep Time: 15 minutes

4 cups cold milk
2 packages (4-serving size each) JELL-O® Chocolate Flavor Instant Pudding & Pie Filling
1 package (12 ounces) pound cake, cut into cubes
¼ cup chocolate syrup or coffee liqueur
1 package (12 ounces) BAKER'S® Semi-Sweet Chocolate Chunks
1 tub (8 ounces) COOL WHIP® Extra Creamy Whipped Topping, thawed

POUR milk into large bowl. Add pudding mixes. Beat with wire whisk 1 minute or until well blended.

PLACE ½ of the cake cubes in large glass serving bowl. Drizzle with ½ of the chocolate syrup. Spread ½ of the pudding over cake in bowl. Sprinkle ½ of the chunks over pudding. Spread with ½ of the whipped topping. Repeat layers. Refrigerate until ready to serve.

Makes 12 servings

Chocolate Passion Layered Dessert

Fresh Fruit Parfaits

Prep Time: 20 minutes   **Refrigerating Time:** 2 hours

1 cup fresh fruit
¾ cup boiling water
1 package (4-serving size) JELL-O® Brand Sugar Free Low
**   Calorie Gelatin Dessert or JELL-O® Brand Gelatin Dessert,**
**   any flavor**
½ cup cold water
**   Ice cubes**
¾ cup thawed COOL WHIP FREE® or COOL WHIP LITE®
**   Whipped Topping**

DIVIDE fruit among 6 parfait glasses.

STIR boiling water into gelatin in medium bowl at least 2 minutes until completely dissolved. Mix cold water and ice cubes to make 1¼ cups. Add to gelatin, stirring until slightly thickened. Remove any remaining ice. Measure ¾ cup of the gelatin; pour into parfait glasses. Refrigerate 1 hour or until set but not firm (gelatin should stick to finger when touched and should mound).

STIR whipped topping into remaining gelatin with wire whisk until smooth. Spoon over gelatin in glasses.

REFRIGERATE 1 hour or until firm. Garnish as desired.

Makes 6 servings

Tip

A parfait refers to the dessert layered in a tall footed clear glass known as a 'parfait glass.'

Luscious Layers

Mocha Pudding Parfaits

Prep Time: 10 minutes

> **1½ cups cold fat free milk**
> **1 tablespoon MAXWELL HOUSE® Instant Coffee**
> **1 package (4-serving size) JELL-O® Chocolate Flavor Fat Free Sugar Free Instant Reduced Calorie Pudding & Pie Filling**
> **1 tub (8 ounces) COOL WHIP FREE® Whipped Topping, thawed, divided**
> **6 reduced fat chocolate wafer cookies, chopped**

POUR milk and coffee into medium bowl. Add pudding mix. Beat with wire whisk 1 minute. Gently stir in ½ of the whipped topping.

SPOON ½ of the pudding mixture evenly into 6 dessert dishes. Sprinkle with chopped cookies. Top with ½ of the remaining whipped topping. Top with remaining pudding mixture. Garnish each serving with a spoonful of remaining whipped topping.

REFRIGERATE until ready to serve.   **Makes 6 servings**

Great Substitute: The coffee can be omitted. Drizzle each serving with 1 teaspoon fat free chocolate syrup for a really indulgent treat!

Cherry Cola Parfaits

Prep Time: 10 minutes   **Refrigerating Time:** 3 hours

> **2½ cups boiling carbonated cola beverage**
> **2 packages (8-serving size each) or 4 packages (4-serving size each) JELL-O® Brand Cherry Flavor Gelatin Dessert**
> **1 tub (8 ounces) COOL WHIP® Whipped Topping, thawed**

STIR boiling beverage into gelatin in large bowl at least 2 minutes until completely dissolved. Pour into 13×9-inch pan. Refrigerate at least 3 hours or until firm. Dip bottom of pan in warm water about 15 seconds. Cut into ½-inch cubes.

LAYER gelatin cubes and whipped topping, in alternating layers, into 6 dessert glasses. Garnish with additional whipped topping, if desired.

                                            Makes 6 servings

Take a Shortcut: For an even quicker version, pour gelatin directly into 6 dessert glasses; refrigerate 3 hours or until set. Top with whipped topping.

Luscious Layers

JELL-O® Yogurt Parfaits

Prep Time: 10 minutes plus refrigerating

> **2 cups boiling water, divided**
> **1 package (4-serving size) JELL-O® Brand Gelatin Dessert, any red flavor**
> **1 container (8 ounces) BREYERS® Vanilla Lowfat Yogurt, divided**
> **1 cup cold water, divided**
> **1 package (4-serving size) JELL-O® Brand Orange Flavor Gelatin Dessert**

STIR 1 cup boiling water into red gelatin in medium bowl at least 2 minutes or until completely dissolved. Remove ½ cup gelatin to small bowl. Stir in ½ of the yogurt. Stir ½ cup cold water into other bowl. Refrigerate both bowls 15 to 20 minutes or until slightly thickened (consistency of unbeaten egg whites).

SPOON creamy red gelatin mixture evenly into 4 dessert glasses. Refrigerate 10 minutes or until thickened (spoon drawn through leaves a definite impression). Top each with clear red gelatin. Refrigerate until thickened.

MEANWHILE, repeat procedure with orange gelatin and remaining ingredients.

REFRIGERATE 3 hours or until firm.   **Makes 4 servings**

Great Substitute: For a fun holiday treat, substitute Lime Flavor Gelatin Dessert for the Orange Flavor Gelatin Dessert. Garnish each serving with a dollop of thawed COOL WHIP® Whipped Topping.

Luscious Layers

Lemon-Blueberry Pie Cups

Prep Time: 15 minutes   **Refrigerating Time:** 2¼ hours

   6 vanilla wafer cookies
   ¾ cup canned blueberry pie filling
   1 cup boiling water
   **1 package (4-serving size) JELL-O® Brand Lemon Flavor Gelatin
      Dessert**
   ¾ cup cold water
   **½ tub (8 ounces) COOL WHIP® Whipped Topping, thawed,
      divided**

PLACE one vanilla wafer on bottom of each of 6 dessert cups. Top each wafer with 2 tablespoons pie filling. Set aside.

STIR boiling water into gelatin in large bowl at least 2 minutes until completely dissolved.

STIR in cold water. Refrigerate 10 to 15 minutes or until mixture is slightly thickened (consistency of unbeaten egg whites). Stir in ½ of the whipped topping until well blended. Spoon over pie filling in cups.

REFRIGERATE 2 hours or until firm. Garnish with remaining whipped topping, if desired.   **Makes 6 servings**

Great Substitutes: Try using cherry or pineapple pie filling instead of the blueberry pie filling.

Serving Suggestion: Garnish each serving with fresh berries, if desired.

Luscious Layers

Black & White Banana Pudding

Prep Time: 20 minutes plus refrigerating

- 1¾ **cups cold milk**
- 1 **package (4-serving size each) JELL-O® Chocolate Flavor Instant Pudding & Pie Filling**
- 24 **NILLA® Chocolate Wafers or NILLA® Wafers**
- 1 **large banana, sliced**
- 1 **tub (8 ounces) COOL WHIP® Whipped Topping, thawed Finely chopped chocolate or sprinkles (optional)**

POUR milk into large bowl. Add pudding mix. Beat with wire whisk 2 minutes or until well blended. Let stand 5 minutes.

ARRANGE ½ of the cookies on bottom of 1- to 1½-quart serving bowl. Top with ½ of the pudding, ½ of the banana slices and ½ of the whipped topping. Repeat layers.

REFRIGERATE 3 hours or until ready to serve. Just before serving, garnish with chopped chocolate and additional banana slices dipped in lemon juice to prevent darkening, if desired.   **Makes 4 to 6 servings**

Citrus Parfaits

Prep Time: 10 minutes   **Refrigerating Time:** 4 hours

- 2 **cups boiling water, divided**
- 1 **package (4-serving size) JELL-O® Brand Lime Flavor Gelatin Dessert**
- 1 **package (4-serving size) JELL-O® Brand Lemon Flavor Gelatin Dessert**
- 2 **cups cold apple juice, divided**
- 1 **tub (8 ounces) COOL WHIP® Whipped Topping, thawed**

STIR 1 cup boiling water into each flavor of gelatin in separate bowls at least 2 minutes until completely dissolved. Stir 1 cup cold juice into each bowl. Pour into separate 9×9-inch pans.

REFRIGERATE 4 hours or until firm. Cut each flavor into ½-inch cubes. Layer, alternating with flavors of gelatin cubes and whipped topping, into 8 dessert glasses. Garnish with additional whipped topping and berries, if desired. Store leftover dessert in refrigerator.   **Makes 8 servings**

JELL-O®
Cool & Creamy Collection

Berry Squares

Prep Time: 10 minutes

- **1 package (12 ounces) pound cake, cut into 10 slices**
- **3 tablespoons orange juice**
- **2 pints fresh seasonal berries (strawberries, raspberries or blueberries)**
- **2 tablespoons sugar**
- **2½ cups cold milk**
- **2 packages (4-serving size each) JELL-O® Vanilla or Lemon Flavor Instant Pudding & Pie Filling**
- **1 tub (8 ounces) COOL WHIP® Whipped Topping, thawed, divided**

ARRANGE cake slices in bottom of 13×9-inch pan. Drizzle cake with juice. Top with berries; sprinkle with sugar.

POUR milk into large bowl. Add pudding mixes. Beat with wire whisk 1 minute or until well blended. Gently stir in 1 cup of the whipped topping. Spoon mixture over berries in pan. Top with remaining whipped topping.

REFRIGERATE until ready to serve or overnight. Garnish as desired.

Makes 15 servings

Berry Square

Chocolate Swirl Cheesecake

Prep Time: 15 minutes   **Refrigerating Time:** 1 hour

1 package (11.1 ounces) JELL-O® No Bake Real Cheesecake
2 tablespoons sugar
1 tablespoon water
6 tablespoons butter or margarine, melted
2 squares BAKER'S® Semi-Sweet Baking Chocolate
1⅔ cups cold milk, divided

STIR Crust Mix, sugar, water and melted butter thoroughly with fork in 9-inch pie plate until crumbs are well moistened. First press firmly against side of pie plate, using finger or measuring cup to shape edge. Press remaining crumbs firmly onto bottom, using measuring cup.

MICROWAVE chocolate and 2 tablespoons of the milk in small microwavable bowl on HIGH 1½ minutes or until chocolate is almost melted. Stir until chocolate is completely melted; cool slightly.

BEAT remaining milk and Filling Mix with electric mixer on lowest speed until blended. Beat on medium speed 3 minutes. (Filling will be thick.) Stir ¼ cup of the filling into melted chocolate until well blended. Spoon remaining filling into crust. Place spoonfuls of chocolate mixture over filling in crust. Cut through cheesecake filling with knife several times to marbleize.

REFRIGERATE at least 1 hour. Garnish as desired.   **Makes 8 servings**

Tip

Cheesecake dates back to the Roman Empire days and still remains one of the most popular desserts of all time.

Fruity JELL-O® Cake

Prep Time: 15 minutes   **Bake Time:** 55 minutes

- **2 cups chopped strawberries**
- **1 can (20 ounces) crushed pineapple, drained**
- **1 package (8-serving size) or 2 packages (4-serving size each) JELL-O® Brand Strawberry Flavor Gelatin**
- **3 cups miniature marshmallows**
- **1 package (2-layer size) white cake mix**
- **2 eggs**

HEAT oven to 350°F.

ARRANGE fruit on bottom of 13×9-inch pan. Sprinkle with gelatin. Cover with marshmallows.

PREPARE cake mix as directed on package, omitting oil and using 2 eggs and water as specified. Spread batter over mixture in pan.

BAKE 50 to 55 minutes. Remove to rack; cool 15 minutes. Serve warm with thawed COOL WHIP Whipped Topping, if desired.   **Makes 24 servings**

No Bake Cappuccino Cheesecake

Prep Time: 15 minutes   **Refrigerating Time:** 1 hour

- **1 package (11.1 ounces) JELL-O® No Bake Real Cheesecake**
- **2 tablespoons sugar**
- **⅓ cup butter or margarine, melted**
- **2 teaspoons MAXWELL HOUSE® Instant Coffee**
- **1½ cups cold milk**
- **¼ teaspoon ground cinnamon**

MIX crumbs, sugar and butter thoroughly with fork in 9-inch pie plate until crumbs are well moistened. Press firmly against side of pie plate first, using finger or large spoon to shape edge. Press remaining crumbs firmly onto bottom, using measuring cup.

DISSOLVE coffee in milk. Beat milk mixture, filling mix and cinnamon with electric mixer on low speed until blended. Beat on medium speed 3 minutes. (Filling will be thick.) Spoon into crust.

REFRIGERATE at least 1 hour.   **Makes 8 servings**

Luscious Lemon Poke Cake

Prep Time: 30 minutes   **Refrigerating Time:** 4 hours

> **2 baked 8- or 9-inch round white cake layers, cooled
>   completely**
> **2 cups boiling water**
> **1 package (8-serving size) or 2 packages (4-serving size each)
>   JELL-O® Brand Lemon Flavor Gelatin Dessert**
> **1 tub (8 or 12 ounces) COOL WHIP® Whipped Topping, thawed**

PLACE cake layers, top sides up, in 2 clean 8- or 9-inch round cake pans. Pierce cake with large fork at ½-inch intervals.

STIR boiling water into gelatin in medium bowl at least 2 minutes until completely dissolved. Carefully pour 1 cup of the gelatin over 1 cake layer. Pour remaining gelatin over second cake layer. Refrigerate 3 hours.

DIP 1 cake pan in warm water 10 seconds; unmold onto serving plate. Spread with about 1 cup of the whipped topping. Unmold second cake layer; carefully place on first cake layer. Frost top and side of cake with remaining whipped topping.

REFRIGERATE at least 1 hour or until ready to serve. Decorate as desired.

Makes 12 servings

Rocky Road Icebox Cake

Prep Time: 15 minutes plus freezing

3½ cups JET-PUFFED® Miniature Marshmallows, divided
2 tablespoons milk
3 cups half-and-half or milk
2 packages (4-serving size each) JELL-O® Chocolate Flavor Instant Pudding & Pie Filling
1 tub (8 ounces) COOL WHIP® Whipped Topping, thawed, divided
5 or more whole HONEY MAID® Honey Grahams, broken into pieces
1 jar (11.75 ounces) hot fudge topping
1 cup PLANTERS COCKTAIL® Peanuts

LINE 9×5-inch loaf pan with foil extending over edges to form handles. Spray foil with no stick cooking spray.

MICROWAVE 3 cups marshmallows in medium microwavable bowl with 2 tablespoons milk 1 to 2 minutes or until almost melted. Stir until completely melted; cool.

POUR half-and-half into large bowl. Add pudding mixes. Beat with wire whisk 2 minutes or until well blended. (Mixture will be thick.) Gently stir in 1 cup whipped topping. Stir remaining whipped topping into cooled marshmallows.

LINE bottom of prepared pan with ⅓ of the honey graham crackers to form crust. Spread with ⅓ jar of hot fudge topping. Sprinkle with ⅓ cup peanuts. Spoon ½ of the pudding mixture over peanuts. Spoon ½ of the marshmallow mixture over pudding. Smooth with spatula. Repeat layers. Freeze at least 4 hours or until firm. **Makes 8 to 10 servings**

How To Serve: Lift dessert from pan, using foil as handles, onto cutting board. Remove foil. Let stand at room temperature 10 minutes before slicing. Top dessert with remaining peanuts, marshmallows and honey graham crackers. Drizzle remaining hot fudge sauce on top. Run knife under hot water and dry with towel for easier cutting.

Tropical Cake Squares

Prep Time: 15 minutes   **Refrigerating Time:** 4½ hours

1½ cups boiling water
**1 package (8-serving size) or 2 packages (4-serving size each)
    JELL-O® Brand Orange Flavor Gelatin**
2 cups cold pineapple orange juice or orange juice
1 package (12 ounces) pound cake, cut into 10 to 12 slices
1 package (8 ounces) PHILADELPHIA® Cream Cheese, softened
¼ cup sugar
1 tub (8 ounces) COOL WHIP® Whipped Topping, thawed
2 cans (15¼ ounces each) fruit cocktail, drained

STIR boiling water into gelatin in large bowl at least 2 minutes until completely dissolved. Stir in cold juice. Refrigerate about 1½ hours or until thickened (spoon drawn through leaves definite impression). Meanwhile, line 13×9-inch pan with pound cake slices, filling any holes with cake pieces.

BEAT cream cheese and sugar in large bowl until smooth. Gently stir in whipped topping. Spread evenly over crust. Top with fruit. Spoon thickened gelatin over cream cheese layer and fruit.

REFRIGERATE 3 hours or until firm.   **Makes 15 servings**

Tip

Easily thaw an unopened 8-ounce tub
COOL WHIP® Whipped Topping in the
refrigerator for 4 hours. Do not thaw
in microwave.

Maple Praline Cheesecake

Prep Time: 15 minutes plus refrigerating

> 1 package (11.1 ounces) JELL-O® Brand No Bake Real
>   Cheesecake
> 2 tablespoons sugar
> 6 tablespoons butter or margarine, melted
> 1 tablespoon water
> 1⅓ cups cold milk
> ½ cup maple syrup
> 1 cup PLANTERS® Pecan Halves or Pieces
> 1 cup firmly packed brown sugar
> 1 egg, beaten

HEAT oven to 350°F.

STIR Crust Mix, sugar, butter and water thoroughly in 8- or 9-inch square baking pan until crumbs are well moistened. Firmly press crumbs onto bottom of pan, using small measuring cup.

POUR milk into large bowl. Add Filling Mix and syrup. Beat with electric mixer on lowest speed until blended. Beat on medium speed 3 minutes. (Filling will be thick.) Spoon over crust.

REFRIGERATE at least 1 hour or until set.

MIX pecans, brown sugar and beaten egg, stirring until well combined. Pour into greased 13×9-inch baking pan. Bake 10 to 12 minutes or until browned and crunchy; cool. Using spatula, loosen nut mixture from pan and chop into small pieces. Just before serving, sprinkle over cheesecake. Cut cheesecake into squares.   **Makes 8 servings**

Easy Cappuccino Cake

Prep Time: 25 minutes

> **1 package (2-layer size) white cake mix**
> **4 tablespoons MAXWELL HOUSE® Instant Coffee, divided**
> **¼ cup milk plus 1 tablespoon milk**
> **4 squares BAKER'S® Semi-Sweet Baking Chocolate, melted**
> **2 tubs (8 ounces each) COOL WHIP® Whipped Topping,**
> **thawed, divided**

HEAT oven to 350°F.

PREPARE and bake cake mix as directed on package for 8- or 9-inch round pans, adding 2 tablespoons instant coffee to cake mix.

POUR ¼ cup milk and 1 tablespoon instant coffee into small bowl, stirring until coffee is dissolved. Slowly stir into melted chocolate until smooth. Cool completely. Gently stir in 1 tub of whipped topping. Refrigerate 20 minutes, or until well chilled.

MEANWHILE, mix 1 tablespoon milk and 1 tablespoon coffee until dissolved. Gently stir into remaining tub of whipped topping.

COVER one cake layer with chocolate mixture. Place second cake layer on top. Frost top and side of cake with coffee-flavored whipped topping. Refrigerate until ready to serve. **Makes 14 servings**

Variation: If desired, omit the coffee for a delicious plain chocolate-filled layer cake.

Down Home Sour Cream Cheesecake

Prep Time: 15 minutes plus refrigerating

> 1 package (11.1 ounces) JELL-O® No Bake Real Cheesecake
> 2 tablespoons sugar
> 6 tablespoons butter or margarine, melted
> 1 tablespoon water
> 1 cup cold milk
> ½ cup sour cream
> 2 teaspoons grated lemon peel
> Lemon Sauce (optional)

STIR Crust Mix, sugar, butter and water thoroughly in 9-inch pie plate until crumbs are well moistened. First, firmly press crumbs against side of pie plate, using measuring cup or large spoon to shape edge. Next, firmly press remaining crumbs onto bottom.

POUR milk into large bowl. Add Filling Mix and sour cream. Beat with electric mixer on lowest speed until blended. Beat on medium speed 3 minutes. (Filling will be thick.) Gently stir in lemon peel and mix until completely blended. Spoon over crust.

REFRIGERATE at least 1 hour or until set. To serve, dip bottom of pan in hot water 30 seconds for easy cutting and serving. Serve with Lemon Sauce (recipe follows).   **Makes 8 servings**

Lemon Sauce: Pour 1 cup cold milk into large bowl. Add 1 package (4-serving size) JELL-O® Lemon Flavor Instant Pudding & Pie Filling. Beat with wire whisk 2 minutes or until well blended. Whisk in 3 tablespoons lemon juice.

Special Extra: Garnish with thawed COOL WHIP® Whipped Topping and lemon slices.

Chocolate Toffee Bar Dessert

Prep Time: 20 minutes   **Bake Time:** 10 minutes
Refrigerating Time: 3 hours

> **1 cup flour**
> **½ cup pecans, toasted and finely chopped**
> **¼ cup sugar**
> **½ cup (1 stick) butter or margarine, melted**
> **1 cup toffee bits, divided**
> **2 cups cold milk**
> **2 packages (4-serving size each) JELL-O® Chocolate Flavor Instant Pudding & Pie Filling**
> **1 tub (8 ounces) COOL WHIP® Whipped Topping, thawed, divided**

HEAT oven to 400°F.

MIX flour, pecans, sugar, butter and ½ cup of the toffee bits in large bowl until well mixed. Press firmly onto bottom of 13×9-inch pan. Bake 10 minutes or until lightly browned. Cool.

POUR milk into large bowl. Add pudding mixes. Beat with wire whisk 1 minute or until well blended. Spread 1½ cups pudding on bottom of crust.

GENTLY stir ½ of the whipped topping into remaining pudding. Spread over pudding in pan. Top with remaining whipped topping. Sprinkle with remaining toffee bits.

REFRIGERATE 3 hours or overnight.   **Makes 15 servings**

Great Substitute: JELL-O Butterscotch Flavor Instant Pudding can be substituted for Chocolate Flavor with delicious results.

White Chocolate Cheesecake

Prep Time: 15 minutes   **Refrigerating Time:** 1 hour

> 1 package (11.1 ounces) JELL-O® No Bake Real Cheesecake
> ⅓ cup butter or margarine, melted
> 2 tablespoons sugar
> 1½ cups cold milk
> 1 package (6 squares) BAKER'S® Premium White Baking
>   Chocolate Squares, melted
> 2 squares BAKER'S® Semi-Sweet Baking Chocolate, melted
>   (optional)

MIX Crust Mix, butter and sugar thoroughly with fork in 9-inch pie plate until crumbs are well moistened. Press firmly against side of pie plate first, using finger or large spoon to shape edge. Press remaining crumbs firmly onto bottom of pie plate using measuring cup.

BEAT milk and Filling Mix with electric mixer on low speed until blended. Beat on medium speed 3 minutes. (Filling will be thick.) Reserve about 3 tablespoons melted white chocolate for garnish, if desired. Stir remaining melted white chocolate into filling mixture. Spoon into crust. Drizzle with reserved melted white chocolate and melted semi-sweet chocolate, if desired.

REFRIGERATE at least 1 hour, if desired.   **Makes 8 servings**

No Bake Pineapple-Ginger Cheesecake Squares

Prep Time: 10 minutes   **Refrigerating Time:** 1 hour

- 1 package (11.1 ounces) JELL-O® No Bake Real Cheesecake
- 2 tablespoons sugar
- 1 tablespoon water
- 6 tablespoons butter or margarine, melted
- 1½ teaspoons ground ginger
- 1 can (20 ounces) crushed pineapple in juice, well drained, divided
- 1½ cups cold milk
- 1 teaspoon grated lemon peel

MIX Crust Mix, sugar, water, butter and ginger thoroughly with fork in 9×9-inch pan until crumbs are well moistened. Reserve 2 tablespoons. Press firmly onto bottom of pan using dry measuring cup. Spread ½ of the pineapple on the crust.

BEAT milk, Filling Mix and lemon peel with electric mixer on low speed until blended. Beat on medium speed 3 minutes. (Filling will be thick.) Spoon over pineapple in crust.

REFRIGERATE at least 1 hour. Top with remaining pineapple and reserved crumbs. Store leftover cheesecake, covered, in refrigerator.

Makes 8 servings

Great Substitute: Orange peel can be substituted for lemon peel.

Cool & Creamy Collection

Pinwheel Cake and Cream

Prep Time: 15 minutes

- **2 cups cold milk**
- **1 package (4-serving size) JELL-O® Vanilla or French Vanilla Flavor Instant Pudding & Pie Filling**
- **1 cup thawed COOL WHIP® Whipped Topping**
- **1 small peach or nectarine, chopped**
- **1 teaspoon grated orange peel**
- **1 package (12 ounces) pound cake, cut into slices**
- **2 cups summer fruits, such as sliced peaches, nectarines or plums; seedless grapes; strawberries, raspberries or blueberries**

POUR milk into large bowl. Add pudding mix. Beat with wire whisk 1 minute. Gently stir in whipped topping, chopped peach and grated peel.

ARRANGE pound cake slices on serving plate. Spoon pudding mixture evenly over cake. Top with fruits. Serve immediately or cover and refrigerate until ready to serve.   **Makes 10 servings**

Miniature Cheesecakes

Prep Time: 15 minutes   **Refrigerating Time:** 1 hour

- **1 package (11.1 ounces) JELL-O® No Bake Real Cheesecake**
- **2 tablespoons sugar**
- **⅓ cup butter or margarine, melted**
- **1½ cups cold milk**
- **2 squares BAKER'S® Semi-Sweet Baking Chocolate, melted (optional)**

MIX crumbs from mix, sugar and butter thoroughly with fork in medium bowl until crumbs are well moistened. Press onto bottoms of 12 paper-lined or foil-lined muffin cups.

BEAT milk and filling mix with electric mixer on low speed until blended. Beat on medium speed 3 minutes. (Filling will be thick.) Spoon over crumb mixture in muffin cups. Drizzle with melted chocolate, if desired.

REFRIGERATE at least 1 hour or until ready to serve. Garnish as desired.
                                                               Makes 12 servings

Layered Chocolate Cheesecake Squares

Prep Time: 20 minutes   **Refrigerating Time:** 1 hour

> **1 package (9.2 ounces) JELL-O® No Bake Chocolate Silk Pie**
> **1 package (11.1 ounces) JELL-O® No Bake Real Cheesecake**
> **½ cup (1 stick) butter or margarine, melted**
> **1⅔ cups cold milk**
> **1½ cups cold milk**

MIX crumbs from both packages and butter thoroughly with fork in medium bowl until crumbs are well moistened. Press firmly onto bottom of foil-lined 13×9-inch pan.

PREPARE Chocolate Silk Pie and Cheesecake fillings, separately, as directed on each package. Spread chocolate filling evenly over crust; top with cheesecake filling.

REFRIGERATE at least 1 hour. Garnish as desired.   **Makes 15 servings**

Layered Chocolate Cheesecake Square

JELL-O®
BRAND

Piece of 'Pie-Fection'

White Chocolate-Hazelnut Pie

Prep Time: 15 minutes plus refrigerating

2 cups cold milk

2 packages (4-serving size each) JELL-O® White Chocolate Flavor or other Chocolate Flavor Instant Pudding Pie Filling

1 envelope (.64 ounces) GENERAL FOODS INTERNATIONAL COFFEES® Hazelnut Flavor (about 2 tablespoons)

1 tub (8 ounces) COOL WHIP® Whipped Topping, thawed, divided

1 prepared chocolate flavor or graham cracker crumb crust (6 ounces or 9 inches)

POUR milk into medium bowl. Add pudding mixes and flavored instant coffee. Beat with wire whisk 1 minute or until well blended. (Mixture will be thick.) Gently stir in ½ of the whipped topping. Spoon evenly into crust. Spread remaining whipped topping over pudding in crust.

REFRIGERATE 3 hours or until set. Garnish as desired.

Makes 8 servings

Spicy Apple Tart

Prep Time: 15 minutes plus refrigerating

   4 cups thinly sliced peeled Granny Smith apples
   ⅔ cup sugar
   ¾ cup apple juice or water
   ½ teaspoon ground cinnamon
   2 tablespoons cornstarch
   ¼ cup cold water
   1 package (4-serving size) JELL-O® Brand Lemon Flavor Gelatin
   1 HONEY MAID® Honey Graham Pie Crust (9 inch)

MIX apples, sugar, apple juice and cinnamon in medium saucepan. Bring to boil on medium-high heat. Cook on medium heat about 5 minutes or until apples are tender. Mix cornstarch and water. Stir into apple mixture. Return to boil; boil 1 minute, stirring constantly. Remove from heat. Stir in gelatin until completely dissolved. Pour into crust.

REFRIGERATE 4 hours or until firm.   **Makes 8 servings**

Great Substitute: Try NILLA® Pie Crust (9 inch) instead of HONEY MAID® Honey Graham Pie Crust.

Serving Suggestion: Garnish with thawed COOL WHIP® Whipped Topping.

Piece of 'Pie-Fection'

No Bake Frozen Chocolate Indulgence

Prep Time: 15 minutes plus freezing

> 1 package (11.4 ounces) JELL-O® No Bake Chocolate Lover's Dessert
> 6 tablespoons butter or margarine, melted
> 1⅓ cups cold milk
> ¾ cup raspberry preserves
> 1 tub (8 ounces) EXTRA CREAMY COOL WHIP® Whipped Topping or COOL WHIP® Whipped Topping

STIR Crust Mix and butter thoroughly in 9-inch pie plate until crumbs are well moistened. First, firmly press crumbs against side of pie plate, using measuring cup or large spoon to shape edge. Next, firmly press remaining crumbs onto bottom.

POUR milk into large bowl. Add Filling Mix. Beat with electric mixer on lowest speed until blended. Beat on medium speed 3 minutes. (Filling will be thick.) Spoon into crust. Spread raspberry preserves evenly over filling. Top with whipped topping and drizzle with Topping.

FREEZE at least 4 hours or until firm. To serve, dip bottom of pan in hot water 30 seconds for easy cutting and serving.   **Makes 8 servings**

Great Substitute: JELL-O® No Bake Chocolate Silk Dessert can be substituted for the Chocolate Lover's Dessert by increasing cold milk to 1⅔ cups.

Mini Chocolate Indulgences Treats: Prepare as directed above, pressing prepared crumb mixture onto bottoms of 12 paper-lined muffin cups (about 1 heaping tablespoon per cup). Divide prepared filling among cups. Spread preserves and whipped topping over each dessert. Drizzle with Topping and freeze.

Piece of 'Pie-Fection'

Sparkling Fruit Tart

Prep Time: 15 minutes plus refrigerating

    1 cup boiling water
    1 package (4-serving size) JELL-O® Brand Strawberry Flavor Gelatin
    1 package (10 ounces) frozen strawberries in syrup
    1 can (11 ounces) mandarin orange segments, drained
    1 small banana, sliced
    1 HONEY MAID® Honey Graham Pie Crust (9 inch)

STIR boiling water into gelatin in large bowl at least 2 minutes until completely dissolved. Add frozen strawberries. Stir until strawberries thaw and gelatin becomes slightly thickened (consistency of unbeaten egg whites).

ARRANGE orange and banana slices on bottom crust. Carefully spoon gelatin mixture over fruit.

REFRIGERATE 4 hours or until firm. Garnish with thawed COOL WHIP® Whipped Topping and fresh strawberry fans, if desired.

Makes 8 to 10 servings

Frozen Coffee Pie

Prep Time: 15 minutes plus freezing

    ½ cup hot fudge sauce
    1 prepared chocolate flavor crumb crust (6 ounces or 9 inches)
 1¾ cups cold milk
    2 packages (4-serving size each) JELL-O® Vanilla Flavor Instant Pudding & Pie Filling
    2 tablespoons MAXWELL HOUSE® Instant Coffee, any variety
    1 tub (8 ounces) COOL WHIP® Whipped Topping, thawed

HEAT hot fudge sauce as directed on jar. Pour into crust, tilting to cover bottom. Freeze 5 minutes.

POUR milk into large bowl. Add pudding mixes and instant coffee. Beat with wire whisk 1 minute or until well blended. Gently stir in whipped topping. Spoon into crust.

FREEZE 4 hours or until firm. Remove from freezer. Let stand 10 minutes before serving. Garnish with additional whipped topping, if desired.

Makes 8 servings

Piece of 'Pie-Fection'

Cookies & Creme Café Pie

Prep Time: 15 minutes plus refrigerating

- **1 package (12.6 ounces) JELL-O® No Bake Cookies & Creme Dessert**
- **⅓ cup butter or margarine, melted**
- **1 ⅓ cups cold milk**
- **¼ cup GENERAL FOODS INTERNATIONAL COFFEE®, Suisse Mocha Flavor, Vanilla Café Flavor or Irish Cream Café Flavor**

STIR Crust Mix and butter thoroughly with spoon in medium bowl until crumbs are well moistened. Press onto bottom and up side of 9-inch pie plate.

POUR cold milk into large bowl. Add Filling Mix and coffee. Beat with electric mixer on low speed 30 seconds. Beat on high speed 3 minutes. Do not underbeat.

RESERVE ½ cup of the crushed cookies. Gently stir remaining crushed cookies into filling until well blended. Spoon mixture into prepared pie crust. Top with reserved cookies. Refrigerate 4 hours or until firm, or freeze 2 hours to serve frozen.

Makes 8 servings

5-Minute Double Layer Pie

Prep Time: 5 minutes

- **1 ¼ cups cold milk**
- **2 packages (4-serving size each) JELL-O® Instant Pudding, Chocolate Flavor, Lemon Flavor or other flavor**
- **1 tub (8 ounces) COOL WHIP® Whipped Topping, thawed, divided**
- **1 prepared graham cracker crumb crust or chocolate pie crust (6 ounces or 9 inches)**

BEAT milk, pudding mixes and ½ of whipped topping in medium bowl with wire whisk 1 minute (mixture will be thick). Spread in crust.

SPREAD remaining whipped topping over pudding layer in crust. Refrigerate until ready to serve.

Makes 8 servings

Piece of 'Pie-Fection'

Layer After Layer Lemon Pie

Prep Time: 20 minutes plus refrigerating

    ⅓ cup strawberry jam
    1 HONEY MAID® Honey Graham Pie Crust (9 inch)
    4 ounces PHILADELPHIA® Cream Cheese, softened
    1 tablespoon sugar
    1 tub (8 ounces) COOL WHIP® Whipped Topping, thawed,
        divided
  1½ cups cold milk or half-and-half
    2 packages (4-serving size each) JELL-O® Lemon Flavor Instant
        Pudding & Pie Filling
    2 teaspoons grated lemon peel

SPREAD jam gently onto bottom of pie crust. Mix cream cheese and sugar in large bowl with wire whisk until smooth. Gently stir in ½ of the whipped topping. Spread on top of jam.

POUR milk into large bowl. Add pudding mixes and lemon peel. Beat with wire whisk 1 minute. (Mixture will be thick.) Gently stir in remaining whipped topping. Spread over cream cheese layer.

REFRIGERATE 4 hours or until set. Garnish with additional whipped topping, if desired.   **Makes 8 servings**

Hint: Soften unwrapped cream cheese in microwave on HIGH 15 to 20 seconds.

Tip

For an extra-special fruity flavor, spread 1 cup strawberries over jam on bottom of crust; proceed as above.

Piece of 'Pie-Fection'

Frozen Black-Bottom-Peanut Butter Pie

Prep Time: 10 minutes plus freezing

    37 RITZ® Crackers
     6 tablespoons butter or margarine, melted
    ⅓ cup hot fudge dessert topping, heated slightly to soften
     1 cup creamy peanut butter
     1 cup cold milk
     1 package (4-serving size) JELL-O® Vanilla or Chocolate Flavor
        Instant Pudding & Pie Filling
     1 tub (8 ounces) COOL WHIP® Whipped Topping, thawed
        Chopped PLANTERS® Peanuts (optional)

CRUSH crackers in zipper-style plastic bag with rolling pin or in food processor. Mix cracker crumbs and butter. Press onto bottom and up side of 9-inch pie plate; chill. Carefully spread fudge topping over crust.

BEAT peanut butter and milk in large bowl with wire whisk until blended. Add pudding mix. Beat with wire whisk 2 minutes or until well blended. Stir in ½ tub whipped topping. Spoon into crust. Spread remaining whipped topping over top.

FREEZE 4 hours. Sprinkle with chopped PLANTERS Peanuts.

Makes 8 servings

Great Substitute: Try using chunky peanut butter instead of creamy for extra peanut flavor.

Piece of 'Pie-Fection'

Summer Berry Pie

Prep Time: 20 minutes plus refrigerating

- ¾ **cup sugar**
- 3 **tablespoons cornstarch**
- 1½ **cups water**
- 1 **package (4-serving size) JELL-O® Brand Gelatin Dessert, any red flavor**
- 1 **cup blueberries**
- 1 **cup raspberries**
- 1 **cup sliced strawberries**
- 1 **prepared graham cracker crumb crust (6 ounces)**
- 2 **cups thawed COOL WHIP® Whipped Topping**

MIX sugar and cornstarch in medium saucepan. Gradually stir in water until smooth. Stirring constantly, cook on medium heat until mixture comes to boil; boil 1 minute. Remove from heat. Stir in gelatin until completely dissolved. Cool to room temperature. Stir in berries. Pour into crust.

REFRIGERATE 3 hours or until firm. Top with whipped topping.

Makes 8 servings

Orange Citrus Pie

Prep Time: 15 minutes plus refrigerating

- 1 **cup boiling water**
- 1 **package (4-serving size) JELL-O® Brand Orange Flavor Gelatin**
- 1 **tub (8 ounces) COOL WHIP® Whipped Topping, thawed, divided**
- 1 **NILLA® Pie Crust (9 inch)**
- 1½ **cups cut-up fresh fruit, or canned fruit, drained**

STIR boiling water into gelatin in large bowl at least 2 minutes until completely dissolved. Refrigerate about 20 minutes or until slightly thickened (consistency of unbeaten egg whites). Gently stir in 2 cups of the whipped topping. Refrigerate about 15 minutes or until mixture mounds. Spoon into crust.

REFRIGERATE 3 hours or until firm. Just before serving, spread with remaining whipped topping. Garnish with fruit.

Makes 8 servings

Piece of 'Pie-Fection'

Black & White Brownie Bottom Pudding Pie

Prep Time: 15 minutes   **Bake Time:** 25 minutes

> 4 squares BAKER'S® Semi-Sweet Baking Chocolate
> ¼ cup (½ stick) butter or margarine
> ¾ cup sugar
> 2 eggs
> 1 teaspoon vanilla
> ½ cup flour
> 2½ cups cold milk
> 2 packages (4-serving size each) JELL-O® White Chocolate or Vanilla Flavor Instant Pudding & Pie Filling

HEAT oven to 350°F (325°F for glass pie plate).

MICROWAVE chocolate and butter in small microwavable bowl on HIGH 2 minutes or until butter is melted. Stir until chocolate is completely melted.

STIR in sugar, eggs and vanilla. Blend in flour. Spread batter in greased 9-inch pie plate. Bake 25 minutes or until toothpick inserted in center comes out with fudgy crumbs. (Do not overbake.) Lightly press center with bottom of measuring cup or back of spoon to form slight depression. Cool on wire rack.

POUR milk into large bowl. Add pudding mixes. Beat with wire whisk 2 minutes or until well blended. Let stand 2 minutes. Spread over brownie pie. Top with thawed COOL WHIP® Whipped Topping and grated chocolate, if desired. Refrigerate until ready to serve.   **Makes 8 servings**

Great Substitute: For an added crunch, stir in ½ cup chopped nuts after the flour and proceed as directed above.

Piece of 'Pie-Fection'

Triple Berry Spring Pie

Prep Time: 20 minutes plus refrigerating

> 3 cups assorted berries
> 1 prepared graham cracker crumb or shortbread crumb crust
> (6 ounces or 9 inches)
> 1½ cups orange juice
> ½ cup sugar
> 2 tablespoons cornstarch
> 1 package (4-serving size) JELL-O® Brand Gelatin, any red
> flavor
> Thawed COOL WHIP® Whipped Topping, optional

ARRANGE berries in bottom of crust.

MIX juice, sugar and cornstarch in medium saucepan over medium heat. Cook on medium heat, stirring constantly, until mixture comes to boil; boil 1 minute. Remove from heat. Stir in gelatin until completely dissolved. Cool to room temperature. Pour over berries in crust.

REFRIGERATE 3 hours or until firm. Garnish with whipped topping, if desired. Store leftover pie in refrigerator.   **Makes 8 servings**

OREO® Black Forest Pie

Prep Time: 20 minutes plus refrigerating

> 1 package (8 ounces) PHILADELPHIA® Cream Cheese, softened
> 2½ cups cold milk
> 2 packages (4-serving size each) JELL-O® Chocolate Flavor
> Instant Pudding & Pie Filling
> 1 OREO® Pie Crust (9 inch)
> 1 cup cherry pie filling
> 1 cup thawed COOL WHIP® Whipped Topping
> OREO® Crunchies for garnish

BEAT cream cheese in large bowl with electric mixer on medium speed. Gradually beat in milk. Add pudding mixes. Beat on low speed 1 minute. Beat on medium speed 1 minute or until well blended. Spoon into crust.

REFRIGERATE 2 hours or until set. Just before serving, spoon pie filling over pudding. Garnish with whipped topping and crunchies.

Makes 8 servings

Piece of 'Pie-Fection'

Ritzy Banana Cream Pie

Prep Time: 15 minutes plus refrigerating

> **37 RITZ® Crackers**
> **½ cup (1 stick) butter or margarine, divided**
> **1 package (6 ounces) BAKER'S® Bittersweet Baking Chocolate, divided**
> **2 large ripe bananas, sliced, divided**
> **1 ½ cups cold milk**
> **2 packages (4-serving size each) JELL-O® Banana Cream Flavor Instant Pudding & Pie Filling**
> **1 tub (8 ounces) COOL WHIP® Whipped Topping, thawed Chocolate-Dipped RITZ® Crackers, for garnish**

CRUSH crackers in zipper-style bag with rolling pin or in food processor. Melt 6 tablespoons butter. Mix cracker crumbs and butter. Press onto bottom and up side of 9-inch pie plate. Refrigerate until firm.

MICROWAVE 4 squares of the chocolate and remaining 2 tablespoons butter in small microwavable bowl on HIGH 2 minutes or until butter is melted. Stir until chocolate is completely melted. Carefully spread chocolate mixture over bottom and side of crust. Arrange ½ of banana slices on bottom and side of chocolate-coated crust.

POUR milk into medium bowl. Add pudding mixes. Beat with wire whisk 2 minutes or until well blended. (Mixture will be thick.) Gently fold in ½ tub whipped topping. Spoon into crust. Top with remaining banana slices. Spread remaining whipped topping on pie.

REFRIGERATE 4 hours or until set. Just before serving, garnish with Chocolate-Dipped RITZ® Crackers.   **Makes 8 servings**

Chocolate-Dipped RITZ® Crackers: Microwave remaining 2 squares chocolate in small microwavable bowl on HIGH 1 to 2 minutes or until chocolate is almost melted. Stir until chocolate is completely melted. Dip each cracker halfway into melted chocolate; let excess chocolate drip off. Place on wax paper-lined cookie sheet. Refrigerate until chocolate is firm.

Great Substitutes: For variety, try JELL-O® Vanilla or Chocolate Flavor Instant Pudding instead of Banana Cream Flavor.

Candy Crunch Pie

Prep Time: 5 minutes plus refrigerating

> **2 cups cold milk**
> **2 packages (4-serving size each) JELL-O® Chocolate or Vanilla Flavor Instant Pudding & Pie Filling**
> **1 tub (8 ounces) COOL WHIP® Whipped Topping, thawed, divided**
> **4 bars (1.5 ounces each) chocolate-covered wafer candy bars, cut into ¼-inch pieces, divided**
> **1 prepared chocolate-flavor crumb crust (6 ounces or 9 inches)**

POUR milk into medium bowl. Add pudding mixes. Beat with wire whisk 1 minute or until well blended. (Mixture will be thick.) Gently stir in ½ of the whipped topping. Reserve ¼ cup of the candy bars. Stir remaining candy into pudding mixture. Spoon into crust.

SPREAD remaining whipped topping over pudding in crust. Sprinkle top with remaining candy.

REFRIGERATE 4 hours or until set.   **Makes 8 servings**

Hint: For best results, place candy bars in freezer or refrigerator prior to cutting.

Great Substitute: Substitute about 1 cup of your favorite candy bar (chopped) for the chocolate-covered wafer pieces.

Note: If making pie in advance, reserve chopped candy bar pieces to garnish just before serving. This will prevent them from becoming soggy in refrigerator.

JELL-O®

Celebratory Creations

Easy Holiday Trifle

Prep Time: 20 minutes plus refrigerating

4 cups boiling water
1 package (8-serving size) or 2 packages (4-serving size each) JELL-O® Brand Orange Flavor Gelatin
1 package (8-serving size) or 2 packages (4-serving size each) JELL-O® Brand Cranberry Flavor Gelatin
2 cups cold water
1 package (10.75 ounces) frozen pound cake, thawed and cubed
1 tub (8 ounces) COOL WHIP® Whipped Topping, thawed
2 cups sliced strawberries (optional)

STIR 2 cups boiling water into each flavor of gelatin in separate bowls at least 2 minutes until completely dissolved. Stir 1 cup cold water into each bowl. Pour into separate 13×9-inch baking pans. Refrigerate 3 hours or until firm. Cut each pan into ½-inch cubes.

PLACE cranberry gelatin cubes in 3½-quart serving bowl or trifle bowl. Layer with cake cubes, ½ of the whipped topping and strawberries. Cover with orange gelatin cubes. Garnish with remaining whipped topping.

REFRIGERATE at least 1 hour or until ready to serve.

Makes 12 to 15 servings

Serving Suggestion: This recipe can also be made in individual glasses as parfaits. Proceed as directed above, alternating gelatin cubes, cake cubes, strawberries and whipped topping.

Celebratory Creations

Layered Mint-Chocolate Loaf

Prep Time: 15 minutes plus refrigerating

> **2 cups boiling water**
> **1 package (8-serving size) or 2 packages (4-serving size each)**
>   **JELL-O® Brand Lime Flavor Gelatin**
> **1 ¼ cups cold water**
> **¼ teaspoon peppermint extract**
> **2 cups thawed COOL WHIP® Whipped Topping**
> **8 OREO® Chocolate Sandwich Cookies, chopped**

STIR boiling water into gelatin in large bowl at least 2 minutes until completely dissolved. Stir in cold water and peppermint extract. Refrigerate about 1½ hours or until slightly thickened (consistency of unbeaten egg whites). Gently stir in whipped topping. Carefully spoon ½ of the gelatin mixture into 9×5-inch loaf pan which has been sprayed with no stick cooking spray. Sprinkle with ½ of the cookies. Repeat layers, ending with gelatin mixture.

REFRIGERATE about 4 hours or until firm. Unmold. Garnish with additional whipped topping and cookies, if desired.

Makes 8 to 10 servings

Great Substitute: Omit peppermint extract. Substitute 8 MYSTIC MINT® Chocolate Sandwich Cookies, chopped, for the OREO® Chocolate Sandwich Cookies.

Tip

This recipe easily takes on a holiday look. Simply sprinkle the COOL WHIP® garnish with red sprinkles.

Celebratory Creations

Sparkling Dessert

Prep Time: 15 minutes plus refrigerating

> 1 ½ **cups boiling water**
> 1 **package (8-serving size) or 2 packages (4-serving size each) JELL-O® Brand Sparkling White Grape or Lemon Flavor Gelatin**
> 2 ½ **cups cold seltzer or club soda**
> 1 **cup sliced strawberries**

STIR boiling water into gelatin in large bowl at least 2 minutes until completely dissolved. Stir in cold seltzer. Refrigerate about 1 ½ hours or until thickened (spoon drawn through leaves definite impression).

MEASURE 1 cup thickened gelatin into medium bowl; set aside. Stir strawberries into remaining gelatin. Spoon into champagne glasses or dessert dishes.

BEAT reserved gelatin with electric mixer on high speed until fluffy and about doubled in volume. Spoon over clear gelatin in glasses. Refrigerate 2 hours or until firm.
                                                              Makes 8 servings

JELL-O® & Juice Holiday Mold

Prep Time: 10 minutes plus refrigerating

> 2 ½ **cups boiling water**
> 1 **package (8-serving size) or 2 packages (4-serving size each) JELL-O® Brand Strawberry Flavor Gelatin or any red flavor**
> 1 **cup cold orange juice or cranberry juice cocktail**
> 1 **can (8 ounces) pineapple chunks, drained**
> 1 **can (11 ounces) mandarin orange segments, drained**

STIR boiling water into gelatin in large bowl at least 2 minutes until completely dissolved. Stir in cold juice. Refrigerate about 1 ½ hours or until thickened (spoon drawn through leaves definite impression).

STIR in fruit. Spoon into 6-cup mold or bowl which has been sprayed with no stick cooking spray.

REFRIGERATE 4 hours or until firm. Unmold. Garnish as desired.
                                                              Makes 10 servings

Note: Do not use fresh or frozen pineapple, kiwi, papaya or guava juice. Gelatin will not set.

172

Celebratory Creations

JELL-O® Easy Relish

Prep Time: 15 minutes plus refrigerating

> **2¼ cups orange juice**
> **½ teaspoon ground cinnamon**
> **⅛ teaspoon ground cloves**
> **1 package (4-serving size) JELL-O® Brand Cranberry Flavor Gelatin**
> **1½ cups finely chopped dried fruit and nuts (such as apricots, raisins, dates and PLANTERS® Walnuts)**

STIR juice, cinnamon and cloves in saucepan. Bring to boil; boil 3 minutes. Stir hot liquid into gelatin in large bowl at least 2 minutes until completely dissolved. Refrigerate about 1½ hours or until thickened (spoon drawn through leaves definite impression). Stir in fruit and nut mixture.

REFRIGERATE about 1 hour or until cold. Spoon relish into serving bowl. Serve over ice cream, pound cake or with your holiday meal.

Makes about 3½ cups

Variation: Prepare as directed, substituting JELL-O® Brand Lemon or Orange Flavor Gelatin for the Cranberry Flavor.

Celebratory Creations

Frozen Pumpkin Squares

Prep Time: 15 minutes plus freezing

> **1 cup NABISCO Old Fashioned Ginger Snaps, finely crushed**
> **¼ cup finely chopped PLANTERS® Walnuts**
> **¼ cup (½ stick) butter or margarine, melted**
> **1¼ cups cold milk**
> **2 packages (4-serving size each) JELL-O® Vanilla Flavor Instant Pudding & Pie Filling**
> **1 cup canned pumpkin**
> **1 teaspoon pumpkin pie spice**
> **1 tub (8 ounces) COOL WHIP® Whipped Topping, thawed, divided**

MIX crumbs, walnuts and butter in small bowl. Reserve 2 tablespoons for garnish. Press onto bottom of foil-lined 8-inch square pan. Refrigerate.

POUR milk into large bowl. Add pudding mixes, pumpkin and spice. Beat with wire whisk 2 minutes or until well blended. Gently stir in 2¼ cups of the whipped topping. Spread over crust.

FREEZE 4 hours or until firm. Let stand at room temperature 10 minutes or until dessert can be easily cut. Cut into squares. Garnish with remaining whipped topping and sprinkle with reserved crumbs.   **Makes 9 servings**

Celebratory Creations

Easy Rocky Road Fudge

Prep Time: 15 minutes plus refrigerating

        1 package (6-serving size) JELL-O® Chocolate Flavor Cook
            & Serve Pudding & Pie Filling (not Instant)
     ¼ cup milk
        3 tablespoons butter or margarine
    2¼ cups powdered sugar
      ½ cup chopped PLANTERS® Walnuts
      ½ cup JET-PUFFED® Miniature Marshmallows

STIR pudding mix and milk in medium microwavable bowl with wire whisk
2 minutes or until well blended. Add butter. Microwave on HIGH 1 minute;
stir. Microwave 45 seconds longer or until mixture just starts to boil around
edge. Beat in sugar with electric mixer. Stir in walnuts and marshmallows.
Spread evenly into 8×4-inch foil-lined loaf pan.

REFRIGERATE about 1 hour.   **Makes 32 (1-inch) pieces**

Storage Know-How: Store in tightly covered container in the refrigerator.

Great Substitutes: Use JELL-O® Vanilla Flavor Cook & Serve Pudding
instead of Chocolate Flavor. Replace walnuts and marshmallows with ½ cup
chopped toasted almonds and ½ cup chopped dried mixed fruit bits.

Celebratory Creations

Merry Cherry Holiday Dessert

Prep Time: 20 minutes plus refrigerating

- **1½ cups boiling water**
- **1 package (8-serving size) or 2 packages (4-serving size each) JELL-O® Brand Cherry Flavor Gelatin Dessert, or any red flavor**
- **1½ cups cold water**
- **1 can (21 ounces) cherry pie filling**
- **4 cups angel food cake cubes**
- **3 cups cold milk**
- **2 packages (4-serving size each) JELL-O® Vanilla Flavor Instant Pudding & Pie Filling**
- **1 tub (8 ounces) COOL WHIP® Whipped Topping, thawed**

STIR boiling water into gelatin in large bowl at least 2 minutes until completely dissolved. Stir in cold water and cherry pie filling. Refrigerate about 1 hour or until slightly thickened (consistency of unbeaten egg whites). Place cake cubes in 3-quart serving bowl. Spoon gelatin mixture over cake. Refrigerate about 45 minutes or until set but not firm (gelatin should stick to finger when touched and should mound).

POUR milk into large bowl. Add pudding mixes. Beat with wire whisk 1 minute. Gently stir in 2 cups of the whipped topping. Spoon over gelatin mixture in bowl.

REFRIGERATE 2 hours or until set. Top with remaining whipped topping and garnish as desired. **Makes 16 servings**

Celebratory Creations

Christmas Rainbow Cake

Prep Time: 30 minutes   **Bake Time:** 30 minutes

> 1 package (2-layer size) white cake mix
> 1 package (4-serving size) JELL-O® Brand Lime Flavor Gelatin
> 1 package (4-serving size) JELL-O® Brand Strawberry Flavor Gelatin
> 2 tubs (8 ounces each) COOL WHIP® Whipped Topping, thawed

HEAT oven to 350°F.

PREPARE cake mix as directed on package. Divide batter equally between 2 bowls. Add lime gelatin to one bowl and strawberry gelatin to the other bowl. Stir until well blended. Pour each color batter into separate greased and floured 9-inch round cake pans.

BAKE 25 to 30 minutes or until toothpick inserted in center comes out clean. Cool 10 minutes; remove from pans. Cool to room temperature on wire racks.

SLICE each cooled cake layer in half horizontally. Place 1 lime-flavored cake layer on serving plate; frost with whipped topping. Top with 1 strawberry-flavored cake layer; frost with whipped topping. Repeat layers. Frost top and side of cake with remaining whipped topping.

Makes 10 to 12 servings

Storage Know-How: Store cakes frosted with COOL WHIP® Whipped Topping in the refrigerator.

Hint: Use any two flavors of JELL-O® Brand Gelatin to fit your favorite holiday.

Frozen Pudding Tortoni

Prep Time: 10 minutes plus freezing

> 1⅔ **cups cold half-and-half**
> ½ **teaspoon almond extract**
> 1 **package (4-serving size) JELL-O® Vanilla Flavor Instant Pudding & Pie Filling**
> 2 **cups thawed COOL WHIP® Whipped Topping**
> ¼ **cup drained chopped maraschino cherries (optional)**
> ½ **cup chopped amaretti cookies (Italian almond-flavored cookies) or chopped toasted PLANTERS® Slivered Almonds**

POUR half-and-half and almond extract into large bowl. Add pudding mix. Beat with wire whisk 2 minutes or until well blended. Gently stir in whipped topping. Stir in cherries and chopped cookies. Spoon into individual dessert dishes or paper-lined muffin cups.

FREEZE 3 hours or until firm.   **Makes 8 servings**

Great Substitute: Use JELL-O® Pistachio Flavor Instant Pudding instead of Vanilla Flavor. Garnish each serving with a dollop of thawed COOL WHIP® Whipped Topping and additional chopped amaretti cookies, if desired.

Celebratory Creations

Quick-and-Easy Holiday Trifle

Prep Time: 20 minutes plus refrigerating

3 cups cold milk
2 packages (4-serving size each) JELL-O® Vanilla Flavor Instant
    Pudding & Pie Filling
1 tub (8 ounces) COOL WHIP® Whipped Topping, thawed
1 package (12 ounces) pound cake, cut into ½-inch cubes
¼ cup orange juice
2 cups sliced strawberries

POUR milk into large bowl. Add pudding mixes. Beat with wire whisk 1 minute. Gently stir in 2 cups of the whipped topping.

ARRANGE ½ of the cake cubes in 3½-quart serving bowl. Drizzle with ½ of the orange juice. Spoon ½ of the pudding mixture over cake cubes. Top with strawberries. Layer with remaining cake cubes, orange juice and pudding mixture.

REFRIGERATE until ready to serve. Top with remaining whipped topping, and garnish as desired.

Makes 12 servings

No Bake Eggnog Cheesecake

Prep Time: 15 minutes   **Refrigerating Time:** 1 hour

1 package (11.1 ounces) JELL-O® No Bake Real Cheesecake
2 tablespoons sugar
⅓ cup butter or margarine, melted
1½ cups cold eggnog

MIX Crust Mix, sugar and butter thoroughly with fork in 9-inch pie plate until crumbs are well moistened. Press firmly against side of pie plate first, using finger or large spoon to shape edge. Press remaining crumbs firmly onto bottom, using measuring cup.

BEAT eggnog and Filling Mix with electric mixer on low speed until blended. Beat on medium speed 3 minutes (filling will be thick). Spoon into crust.

REFRIGERATE at least 1 hour.

Makes 8 servings

Index

Index

METRIC CONVERSION CHART

VOLUME MEASUREMENTS (dry)

$^1/_8$ teaspoon = 0.5 mL
$^1/_4$ teaspoon = 1 mL
$^1/_2$ teaspoon = 2 mL
$^3/_4$ teaspoon = 4 mL
1 teaspoon = 5 mL
1 tablespoon = 15 mL
2 tablespoons = 30 mL
$^1/_4$ cup = 60 mL
$^1/_3$ cup = 75 mL
$^1/_2$ cup = 125 mL
$^2/_3$ cup = 150 mL
$^3/_4$ cup = 175 mL
1 cup = 250 mL
2 cups = 1 pint = 500 mL
3 cups = 750 mL
4 cups = 1 quart = 1 L

VOLUME MEASUREMENTS (fluid)

1 fluid ounce (2 tablespoons) = 30 mL
4 fluid ounces ($^1/_2$ cup) = 125 mL
8 fluid ounces (1 cup) = 250 mL
12 fluid ounces (1$^1/_2$ cups) = 375 mL
16 fluid ounces (2 cups) = 500 mL

WEIGHTS (mass)

$^1/_2$ ounce = 15 g
1 ounce = 30 g
3 ounces = 90 g
4 ounces = 120 g
8 ounces = 225 g
10 ounces = 285 g
12 ounces = 360 g
16 ounces = 1 pound = 450 g

DIMENSIONS

$^1/_{16}$ inch = 2 mm
$^1/_8$ inch = 3 mm
$^1/_4$ inch = 6 mm
$^1/_2$ inch = 1.5 cm
$^3/_4$ inch = 2 cm
1 inch = 2.5 cm

OVEN TEMPERATURES

250°F = 120°C
275°F = 140°C
300°F = 150°C
325°F = 160°C
350°F = 180°C
375°F = 190°C
400°F = 200°C
425°F = 220°C
450°F = 230°C

BAKING PAN SIZES

Utensil	Size in Inches/Quarts	Metric Volume	Size in Centimeters
Baking or Cake Pan (square or rectangular)	8×8×2	2 L	20×20×5
	9×9×2	2.5 L	23×23×5
	12×8×2	3 L	30×20×5
	13×9×2	3.5 L	33×23×5
Loaf Pan	8×4×3	1.5 L	20×10×7
	9×5×3	2 L	23×13×7
Round Layer Cake Pan	8×1½	1.2 L	20×4
	9×1½	1.5 L	23×4
Pie Plate	8×1¼	750 mL	20×3
	9×1¼	1 L	23×3
Baking Dish or Casserole	1 quart	1 L	—
	1½ quart	1.5 L	—
	2 quart	2 L	—